WHO ARE YOU?

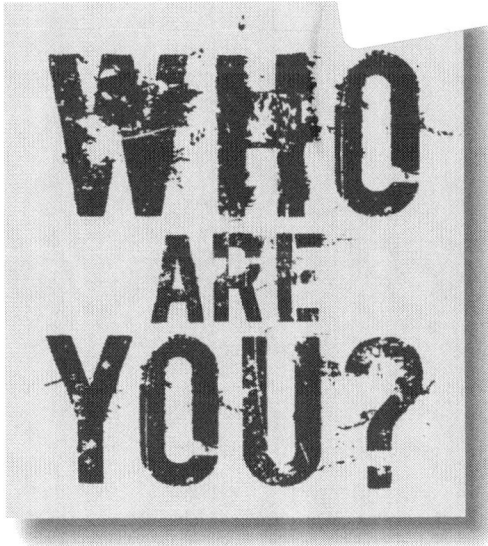

- You Are Born of God
- You Are Forgiven
- You Are Justified
- You Are Created for Explosive and Lasting Change

Who are you?
Copyright © 2019 Craig Seawright

ISBN: 9781688999831

Ministry website: www.seawrightministries.com

All scripture verses are taken from the New King James Version, in the public domain unless stated otherwise.

To my family....

To my beautiful wife Tracey. Thank you for your constant love, grace and strength.

To Reuben, my boy and my best mate.

To Eden Grace, my girl and my princess.

I love you forever.

WHO ARE YOU?

Table of Contents

WHO ARE YOU?

INTRODUCTION

 "Who Are You?" is not a book of mainstream exhortation to be read, but of slipstream theology to be studied. This book is not written with the intention of appealing to as many people as possible within the general Christian demographic. This book was written to fuel the fire of a remnant. A remnant of believers that are already experiencing the early winds of reformation. A remnant of believers that are hearing the call to greater devotion and proximity with the Father. A remnant of believers that are finished with religion and are hungry to experience the goodness of God in the land of living. A remnant of believers that are passionate about becoming the manifestation of the Sons and Daughters of God that all creation is crying out for. My prayer is that you find within this book, a flow of authentic New Covenant Truth, that gives you plenty to meditate upon. I hope and pray that you do not find within this book dry doctrine, but doctrine with a heart-beat and a practical life-giving flow. Doctrine that has not primarily come out of a text book, but out of my personal journey, which is why I thought it best to begin by sharing a little bit of my personal story and journey.

Due to the fact that I grew up within the Northern Ireland conflict (more commonly known as "The Troubles"), I know exactly what it is like to live under threat. My father was shot and killed when I was ten years old. My father's murder was the ultimate eye of the storm for me and my family, a storm that began with a dark cloud of threat. A dark cloud that my family lived under, on a daily basis. In the time leading up to my father's murder, we as a family were reminded of the threat against his life on an almost daily basis. We would have police officers come to our home in order to make us aware that there was a hit out against my father's life. Suspicious cars were spotted outside of our school. When my father went to start our car in the mornings, my mother, two sisters and I would stand at a safe distance whilst my father made sure there were no bombs attached to our car. People would call our home telephone and tell us that they were going to kill my father and us, his family. There was even graffiti on certain walls throughout Belfast letting us know in no uncertain terms of the threat against my father's life. With the dark cloud of threat comes the inevitable arrival of an even darker cloud, called fear.

During the time of the threat against my father's life I had a dream. Most dreams simply come about when we go to bed with a restless and busy mind. However, this dream was most definitely spiritual and most definitely dark and demonic. In the dream, I was in a dark alleyway, with my parents and my two sisters hiding behind an old piece of furniture. The devil then came to the front of the alleyway, pointed at my father and said to me, "I am going to kill your Daddy, then I am going to destroy you and your family." You could ask, how did I know it was the devil and what did he look like? The best way that I can describe it is that seeing seemed unnecessary in the presence of such spiritual darkness. I woke up from this dream, sweating and crying with fear. Two weeks after this dark and disturbing dream, my father was gunned down and killed. What I didn't know and understand then, was that even before that dream, certain wheels had been set in motion, both in the spiritual and physical realm, that would ultimately lead to my father's murder.

In and through that dream, the devil, the father of all lies, had planted his ultimate lie in my mind. That lie being, that he could bring death and destruction in my life as and when he desired to do so. As far as I was concerned, he told me he was going to kill my Daddy, which he did, and so I believed he would go on to carry out the rest of his threat and destroy me and my family. The devil had his ultimate hook in my life. I was truly oppressed and controlled by a spirit of fear. I truly believed that the devil could bring destruction in my life as and when he desired, and so I began to hit the self-destruct button in every area of my life. I saw my life like a car, a car that the devil could crash at will and so I continued to crash the car myself, in a fear driven attempt to at least have some form of control over the steering wheel. Anything that was good in my life, I crashed it as I was truly under the control of fear. On most nights when I closed my eyes to go to sleep, I would see images of my father being shot, or of his coffin being lowered into the ground. On top of this, my father's murder was celebrated by some people within my home city, so much so that a song was made up to mock his death. The words of that song where as follows; "Seawright, got a hole in the head for Christmas and a lot for his family." I would see these words written on walls and even hear them sung, and it was like a knife being twisted on the inside of me. I was full of fear, anger, bitterness, and hatred, all of which only got stronger as I entered into my early teens. I hated how I felt, I hated the fear and the nightmares. I hated being so angry and bitter inside, but most of all, I still really missed my Daddy.

The Whisper

In order to escape, or I should say try and escape it all, I turned to a life of alcohol and drug abuse, which in truth, only brought greater pain and brokenness in my life. However, even in the midst of the darkness God was still there, reaching out to me from His heart of Amazing Grace. Consider the powerful words of David in Psalm 23:6;

Surely goodness and mercy shall follow me All the days of my life

Psalm 23:6 (NKJV)

The word 'mercy' comes from the Hebrew word *checed* (pronounced "hasid"). The word *checed* is mentioned 248 times in the Old Testament and 139 times by David in the Psalms. David was a man after God's own heart because God's heart is a heart of *checed*. *Checed* is the heart force of Heaven. *Checed* is God's obsessive, aggressive, relentless commitment to the divine wellbeing of all humanity. A divine wellbeing that must be consented to, but a divine wellbeing that is toward all humanity, all the same. This is echoed in the powerful words of Matthew 10:30, words that truly capture Gods heart of *checed;*

But the very hairs of your head are all <u>numbered</u>.

Matthew 10:30 (NKJV)

The word 'numbered' comes from the Greek word *arithmeo* and it means counted. I truly love my wife Tracey, but I have never lain awake at night and counted the number of hairs on her head! Think about it, God has counted the very hairs on your head, that's *checed!* Notice, David boldly declares;

'Surely goodness and checed, shall follow me, All the days of my life'

The word 'follow' comes from the Hebrew word *radaph* and it means, to run after or to chase down. I so get this verse, because I know His *checed* followed me and followed me into some extremely dark places. As a young man I would spend a lot of time in paramilitary shebeens (illegal drinking dens). So often within these shebeens I would sense God's presence, something I had experienced many times as a young boy before my father's murder. In that presence, I would hear this continuous voice in my mind, telling me "You don't belong here Craig, this is not who you are." I can remember being up an alleyway, vomiting as a result of my excessive drinking and drug taking, and I heard a voice, a voice that seemed to come from just over my shoulder, a voice that said, "I still want you Craig." I was so confused and, in all honesty, frightened that I was losing my mind.

I was a broken 21-year-old man trying to drink away the 10-year-old boy that just wanted his Daddy back. I was hearing a call to come and lay my pain, hatred and alcoholism at God's feet. I tried, with everything that was within me, to escape and drink away that call. The truth was, I was afraid to come to God with my mess because I was afraid of what I would get in return. But His *checed* followed me and followed me into some extremely dark places. His *checed* hunted me down until I felt like there was nowhere I could hide from His voice that was calling me to come and lay my brokenness at His feet. And so, I did. I came to Him, fell on my knees and presented him with my pain, hatred and alcoholism. And do you know what He gave me in exchange? He gave me a whisper, a whisper that marked my life forever. A whisper that said, "I'll be your Daddy Craig." God gave me, the 21-year-old man that was trying to drink away the 10-year-old boy that just wanted his Daddy back, a whisper. A whisper that came straight from His heart of *checed*. A whisper that epitomises His heart beat of *checed*, that heart beat being His passionate desire to Father us.

The Invitation

Fast forward one year from when I first heard and responded to that whisper and my life has been radically changed. I am free from the fear that controlled me. I am free from the hatred and bitterness that plagued my soul. I have a sense of purpose and destiny in my life. I have a new church family that I love. I have a Pastor and Godly men that I love and look up to. Overall, God had truly brought me out of darkness and into light. It's in this light that I heard a vital invitation from God. That invitation being simply this, "Let me show you who you really are." If the vital whisper that I heard in the darkness was, "I'll be your Daddy", then the vital invitation that I heard in the light was, "Let me show you who you really are."

Around the same time that I received this invitation, God began to speak to me about attending Bible College. Following what I knew to be God's leading, I relocated to Newport, Wales, for my first year of studies and went on to complete my second year in Fort Worth, Texas. During this very special time in my life I received many powerful words of prophesy, from many great men and women of God. Prophetic words communicating that I was carrying revival for Ireland and many other nations. That I was carrying a powerful anointing to preach and teach God's Word, that I would be an influential leader within the body of Christ, that multiple doors would open, that I would preach and teach on multiple platforms and write anointed books.

God had given me what I knew to be a vital invitation. That invitation being, "Let me show you who you really are", and I then automatically assumed that all these prophetic words concerning ministry and what I would do for God was Him showing me who I was. In other words, I took those prophetic words and assumed them as my God given identity and returned home to win Ireland for Jesus.

After returning home, I eventually ended up taking a job as a minimum wage security guard. The job was simple. I was positioned in the reception area of a particular building. In order for people to gain access to this building they had to ring a buzzer. I would then hear the buzzer, make sure I recognised the person, and open the front doors by pressing two small switches located at my desk. I didn't even have to get up off my chair. Outside of these basic duties, I had a large desk and privacy to study and listen to teachings. My plan was simple, I would work this minimum wage security job for a couple of months in preparation for the opening of a great and effectual door of ministry. It was the perfect set up, for 10 hours a day and five days a week, I got to study, listen to teachings, and plan for the ministry. Give it a couple of months and I would be taking Ireland for Jesus.

However, that's not quite how it all worked out. I was there a little longer than a couple of months, 14 years longer to be exact. Within those 14 years I would spend hours and days sitting at that desk, looking at the same four walls, fighting back tears. I was at times overwhelmed with discouragement. There was no revival. There was almost no preaching or teaching opportunities. Almost every ministry endeavour I attempted failed. I didn't know where I fitted within the body of Christ or where I truly belonged. The young dreamer that returned home from Bible College, was dying a long slow death. Yet, every time I planned to leave that job and come out of that place, I would hear God say, "No, I brought you here and I'll tell you when it's time to leave." Then one day, as I sat at my desk, something in me broke. It was early in the morning, before any of the other staff had arrived. I sat down at my desk and the presence of God came upon me so heavily that I put my head on my desk and began to weep. In this weighty presence, God spoke to my heart and said, "Craig, I did not bring you to this place to kill your dreams. I brought you to this place to kill the lie and show you who you really are. I brought you here to kill the lie, that your identity is found in ministry and what you do for me. How many people you preach to, how many books you sell, what leaders you get close to, how many people know your name, who likes you, who applauds you and who accepts you. None of these things are who you are."

I had taken those prophetic words and assumed them as my identity and in making them my identity, I turned my heart away from God and towards success in ministry. God had brought me to that place, in order to bring me to Himself. He wanted my heart, and He wanted it interlocked with His.

He wanted me to be a husband, to my

beautiful wife Tracey, from His heart.

He wanted me to be a Daddy, to my son Reuben

and daughter Eden Grace, from His heart.

He wanted me to be a friend from His heart.

He wanted me to be an authentic minister of

the gospel, from His heart.

He wanted me to write from His heart.

He wanted me to live in peace and be at rest

from His heart.

God had not brought me into a wilderness of discontent in order to abandon me. He had brought me into a wilderness of invitation, in order to woo me. That powerful invitation being, "Let me show you who you really are. It will pull you close to me and that closeness will become the bedrock of your life and ministry. It will cause you to live, move, and have your very being, from my heart of *checed*."

During my teenage years all of my friends would take drugs and drink alcohol, just as I did. However, at a certain time in the evening, their Daddies would come and grab them by the scruff of their necks and give them a firm dose of correction, putting them into their car and taking them home. The next day my friends would all comment on how lucky I was, in that I could sit up all night drinking and taking drugs with no one to bother me. However, what they didn't know was that, when they were all safely tucked up in their beds, I would spend most of my night alone, not just taking drugs and drinking, but crying. What was I crying for? I was crying for a Daddy. Oh how I wished I had a Daddy to come and correct me and take me home out of my mess. You see, my friends saw the absence of correction in my life as a positive, whereas I saw and felt it as a painful absence of love. That's why I so get Hebrews 12:9.

Furthermore, we have had human fathers who corrected us, and we paid them respect. Shall we not much more readily be in subjection to the Father of spirits and live?

Hebrews 12:9 (NKJV)

This book is primarily written from my own personal journey of correction. A journey that has seen Him correct my pride, my selfish ambition, and my religious man-made doctrines that were blinding me to my true identity in Him and stifling my growth as a secure son of God. I am most definitely still on that journey, and my heart in writing this book was not just to give you more doctrine but to give you strength and fuel for your personal journey. Strength and fuel for your personal journey in being Fathered by God. Consider the powerful words contained within Romans 8:14-19, of the Passion Translation;

The mature children of God are those who are moved by the impulses of the Holy Spirit. And you did not receive the "spirit of religious duty," leading you back into the fear of never being good enough. But you have received the "Spirit of full acceptance," enfolding you into the family of God. And you will never feel orphaned, for as He rises up within us, our spirits join Him in saying the words of tender affection, "Beloved Father!" For the Holy Spirit makes God's Fatherhood real to us as <u>He whispers</u> into our innermost being, "You are God's beloved child!" And since we are His true children, we qualify to share all His treasures, for indeed, we are heirs of God Himself. And since we are joined to Christ, we also inherit all that he is and all that he has. We will experience being co- glorified with Him provided that we accept His sufferings as our own. I am convinced that any suffering we endure is less than nothing compared to the magnitude of glory that is about to be unveiled within us. The entire universe is standing on tiptoe, yearning to see the unveiling of God's glorious Sons and Daughters!

Romans 8:14-19 Passion Translation

As you read this book, I encourage you to....

Hear the Whisper - You are the Sons and Daughters of God and you have a Daddy, and

Accept the Invitation – Let Him show you who you really are.

Let Him teach you how to live, move, and have your being from His heart of *checed*, that together, we may be that reformation remnant, and together, we may be the manifestation of the Sons and Daughters of God that all creation is longing for.

Amen.

In "Who Are You?" we will reveal the explosive New Covenant Truths, that;

> You Are Born of God.
>
> You Are Forgiven.
>
> You Are Justified.
>
> You Are Created for Explosive and Lasting Change.

In journeying through these powerful revelations together....

I pray that the Father of Glory, the God of our Lord Jesus Christ, would impart to you the riches of the Spirit of wisdom and the Spirit of revelation to know Him through your deepening intimacy with Him. I pray that the light of God will illuminate the eyes of your imagination, flooding you with light, until you experience the full revelation of the hope of His calling – that is, the wealth of God's glorious inheritances that He finds in us, His holy ones! I pray that you will continually experience the immeasurable greatness of God's power made available to you through faith. Then your lives will be an advertisement of this immense power as it works through you!

Ephesians 1:17-19 Passion Translation

God is love, and he who abides in love abides in God, and God in him.

1 John 4:16

CHAPTER 1

You are Born of God

Before moving into the explosive revelations, covered in Chapters 2 & 3, it is vitally important that we first lay the foundational revelation of your spiritual regeneration. Let's now go on to discover this vital revelation together, keeping in mind that "Who Are You?" is not a book of mainstream exhortation to be read, but of slipstream theology to be carefully studied, contemplated and digested.

"There once was an ugly duckling". Famous lyrics, from a well-known literary fairy tale, by Danish poet and author Hans Christian Anderson. The ugly duckling is the story of a swan whose egg accidentally rolled into the duck's nest. As the so-called ugly duckling struggled to adjust and conform to life in and around the duck pond, it suffered a tragic crisis of identity, causing it to develop a stifling inferiority complex, which in turn caused it to live out a limited and frustrating existence. One day the ugly duckling caught a glance of his reflection in the water and was shocked to discover that he was in fact a beautiful, gracious swan. As he looked upon his true reflection in the mirror of the water, he was liberated from his identity crisis and inferiority complex, eventually going on to take flight with his kindred flock. Speculation suggests that Hans Christian Anderson was the son of Prince Christian Frederik (later King Christian VIII of Denmark), and he found this out some time before he wrote the story. It is widely believed that the swan in the story was a metaphor for Hans Christian Anderson's concealed and later to be revealed royal lineage.

You Are Royalty

The powerful declaration contained within 1 Peter 2:9, confirms our royal lineage as the Sons and Daughters of God.

But you are a chosen generation, a <u>royal</u> priesthood, a holy nation, His own special people, that you may proclaim the praises of Him who called you out of darkness into His marvellous light.

1 Peter 2:9

Surely there is no greater crisis of identity than the one that has spread throughout the body of Christ. A crisis of identity that has caused so many of God's royal Sons and Daughters to develop a stifling inferiority complex, causing them to live out a limited and frustrating existence. I truly believe that the spirit of reformation is stirring within the church. A spirit of reformation that is birthing a systemic exodus from the duck pond of religious Christianity. The erroneous man-made doctrines of self-righteousness have caused God's royal Sons and Daughters to paddle in a duck pond of inferior living. It's time to look into the mirror of God's Word and allow the Spirit of reformation Himself to awaken us to our true identity and inheritance in Christ. It's time for the Sons and Daughters of God to be completely liberated from any form of identity crisis and inferiority complex. It's time to leave the duck pond of religious Christianity behind and soar with our God-ordained kindred flock.

The Mirror that Liberates

The key to the divine liberation of the Sons and Daughters of God is the mirror that liberates. Consider the following declaration contained within 2 Corinthians 3:17-18;

Now the Lord is Spirit, and where the Spirit of the Lord is, there is liberty. But we all, with unveiled face, beholding as in a mirror the glory of the Lord, are being transformed into the same image from glory to glory, just as from the Lord, the Spirit.

2 Corinthians 3:17-18 (New American Standard Bible)

Religious Christianity looks into God's Word as if through a window and admires God from a place of limited inferiority. However, the Spirit of Truth desires for us to look into God's

Word as a mirror. A mirror that reflects our true identity and inheritance in Christ. My prayer for "Who Are You?" is that the Spirit of Truth would use it as a mirror. A mirror that reflects who you truly are in Him. A mirror that liberates you from religious paddling and empowers you to be who you already are.

The Truth That Liberates

Consider the following declaration, recorded in 1 John 4:16;

God is love, and he who abides in love abides in God, and God in him.

1 John 4:16

God is love. He does not simply have love, He is love and everything that He says and does is rooted and grounded in love. Satan is fear. He does not simply have fear, he is fear and everything he says and does is rooted and grounded in fear. And because his primary fear is the divine liberation of the royal Sons and Daughters of God, his primary objective is to undermine and shoot down the truth that liberates, in and through a strategy that is rooted and grounded in the fear of extremes. Consider the outworking of this strategy:

Satan deceives preachers and teachers within the body of Christ to take individual truths hostage to extremes.

Satan then deceives other preachers and teachers within the body of Christ into a wrong response, which sees them not only shoot down the extremes, but the hostage of truth. For example, a preacher on Christian television preaches an extreme message on finances and many other preachers retaliate by not only shooting down the extreme, but shooting down the truth of God's covenant provision. Another example: someone preaches an extreme grace message, and many retaliate by not only shooting down the extreme, but shooting down the hostage that is God's amazing grace.

In other words, the devil births and throws up extremes, in order to kick-start a futile gun battle, with the church caught in the middle, void of the truth that will truly liberate them. A futile gun battle, that results in the royal Sons and Daughters of God living in condemnation, because their preacher is too busy allegedly shooting down the extremes of grace. Broke, because their preacher is busy allegedly shooting down the extremes of prosperity. Sick, because their preacher is busy allegedly shooting down the extremes of healing. In bondage, because their preacher is busy allegedly shooting down the extremes of holiness. Powerless, because their preacher is too busy allegedly shooting down charismatic extremes. Surely the Spirit of reformation is calling on all authentic five-fold ministers, to humble themselves before God and receive His wisdom not to shoot the hostage of truth but to redeem and rescue it. That the royal Sons and Daughters of God would come to truly know the truth and the truth will set them free.

On the outer court of every vital new covenant truth, there are erroneous extremes. My prayer concerning "Who Are You?" is that the Spirit of God would use it, to take you past the outer courts of erroneous extremes and into the inner courts of authentic New Covenant truth; that you would truly grasp the radical truth of your spiritual rebirth in Him; that you would truly grasp the radical truth of your forgiveness in Him and that you would truly grasp the radical truth of your justification in Him.

I believe that when truly grasped and understood, these radical truths will not bring you to a place of passivity and self-indulgence that may well be the fruit of the erroneous outer court extremes. However, the fruit of authentic inner court truth is explosive and lasting change, that will bring about the glorious liberation of the Sons and Daughters of God that all creation is yearning for.

Because the creation itself also will be delivered from the bondage of corruption into the glorious liberty of the children of God.

Romans 8:21

The words of Jesus recorded in John 8:32 affirm truth as the key to our liberation;

And you shall know the truth, and the truth shall make you free.

John 8:32

The word "free" comes from the Greek word *eleutheroo* and it means "to liberate". It is knowing the truth and only knowing that truth that can bring about the glorious liberty of God's royal Sons and Daughters. Let's take a deeper look into the make-up of the truth that liberates.

The Truth that Liberates Came Through Jesus Christ

Jesus came as the only begotten of the Father, as confirmed in John 3:16, and the truth that liberates came with Him, as confirmed in John 1:14:17:

For God so loved the world that He gave His only begotten Son, that whoever believes in Him should not perish but have everlasting life.

John 3:16

And the Word became flesh and dwelt among us, and we beheld His glory, the glory as of the only begotten of the Father, full of grace and truth. John bore witness of Him and cried out, saying, "This was He whom I said, 'He who comes after me is preferred before me, for He was *before me.'" And of His fullness we have all received, and grace for grace. For the law was given through Moses, but grace and <u>truth came through Jesus Christ</u>.*

John 1:14-17

God the Father so loved the world that He gave His only begotten son and the truth that liberates arrived with His only begotten son.

The Truth that Liberates is the Unveiling of the Many Begotten Sons & Daughters of God

The word "truth" comes from the Greek word *aletheia* and it means "uncovered, unveiled and fully revealed". The truth that liberates prior to the death, burial and resurrection of Jesus was the unveiling and full revelation of the only begotten Son of the Father and all His fullness. However, as result of the death, burial and resurrection of Jesus, the truth that liberates is now the unveiling and full revelation of the many begotten Sons and Daughters of God. Consider the additional revelation of the many begotten Sons and Daughters of God, contained within 1 Peter 1:3:

Blessed be the God and Father of our Lord Jesus Christ, who according to His abundant mercy has <u>begotten us</u> again to a living hope through the resurrection of Jesus Christ from the dead.

1 Peter 1:3

Here is the concrete truth: if you have confessed with your mouth the Lord Jesus and believed in your heart that God has raised Him from the dead in accordance with Romans 10:9 and if you have called upon the name of the Lord in accordance with Romans 10:13, you have been begotten again to a living hope through the resurrection of Jesus Christ from the dead. In other words, you are a begotten Son or Daughter of God.

The weighty words contained within Hebrews 2:10 communicate this vital revelation:

For it was fitting for Him, for whom are all things and by whom are all things, in bringing many sons to glory, to make the captain of their salvation perfect through sufferings.

Hebrews 2:10

Praise God! Pre–cross, truth was the unveiling and revealing of the only begotten son; everything He is and has in the Father. However, post–cross, truth is the unveiling and revealing of the many begotten Sons and Daughters; everything that they are and have in the Father. Nowhere is this better confirmed than in the copulative Scripture texts that are John 16:13-15 and Romans 8:14-17. Let's consider these two Scripture texts together and allow the Holy Spirit to marry them as one copulative force:

However, when He, the Spirit of Truth, has come, He will guide you into all truth; for He will not speak on His own authority, but whatever He hears He will speak; and He will tell you things to come. He will glorify Me, for He will take of what is Mine and declare it to you. All things that the Father has are Mine. Therefore I said that He will take of Mine and declare it to you.

John 16:13-15

For as many as are led by the Spirit of God, these are the sons of God. For you did not receive the spirit of bondage again to fear, but you received the Spirit of adoption by whom we cry out, "Abba, Father". The Spirit Himself bears witness with our spirit that we are children of God, and if children, then heirs – heirs of God and joint heirs with Christ, if indeed we suffer with Him, that we may also be glorified together.

Romans 8:14:17

Jesus clearly promised, as recorded in John 16:13-15, that the Spirit of Truth would come and that He would guide us into all truth, by taking everything that belongs to Jesus, in the Father, and declaring it to us. Paul then tells us in Romans 8:14-17 that the Spirit himself bears witness with our spirit that we are children of God, and if children, then heirs – heirs of God and joint heirs with Christ. Praise God, Romans 8:14-17 is John 16:13-15 being fulfilled. The Spirit of Truth, guiding you into all truth, is the Spirit of Truth bearing witness with your spirit that you are a child of God and joint heir with Christ. The hearing of the truth that liberates, is the hearing of who you are and everything that belongs to you, in the Father. The preaching and teaching of the truth that liberates, is the preaching and teaching of who you are and everything that belongs to you, in the Father.

To Know the Truth is to Know Who You Are

Let's look again at the words of Jesus, recorded within John 8:32:

And you shall <u>know the truth</u>, and the truth shall make you free.

John 8:32

Notice, Jesus said, "you shall know the truth, and the truth shall make you free." The word "know" comes from the Greek word *ginosko* and it means "the recognition of truth by personal experience". God greatly desires that you would come to recognise and personally experience the fullness of everything that you are and have, in the Father. In order to recognise and personally experience the fullness of everything that you are and have, in the Father, you must first have a foundational understanding that you are a complex triune being. In other words, you are a complex three-part being, those three parts being clearly defined by Paul in 1 Thessalonians 5:23, as your spirit, soul and body.

Now may the God of peace Himself sanctify you completely; and may your whole spirit, soul and body be preserved blameless at the coming of our Lord Jesus Christ.

1 Thessalonians 5:23

You are a complex three-part being. You are a spirit, you have a soul and you live in a body. Consider the following Scriptures that also clearly differentiate between your spirit, soul and body, beginning with Hebrews 4:12:

For the word of God is living and powerful, and sharper than any two-edged sword, piercing even to the division of soul and spirit, and of joints and marrow…

Hebrews 4:12

The word "piercing" comes from the Greek word *diikneomai* and it means "to penetrate and reach through". The word "division" comes from the Greek word *merismos* and it means "a separation". The Greek word *merismos* comes from the Greek word *merizo* and it means "to part or to apportion". The terms joints and marrow are clear references to the make-up of the physical body. With all this in mind, Hebrews 4:12 could be accurately paraphrased as follows:

For the word of God is living and powerful, sharper than any two-edged sword, penetrating and reaching through the separate portions of your whole being, those separate portions being your soul, and spirit and body.

Hebrews 4:12 (paraphrase)

The words of Paul in 1 Corinthians 14:14 also differentiate between your spirit and your soul:

> *For if I pray in a tongue, my spirit prays, but my understanding is unfruitful.*
>
> *1 Corinthians 14:14*

The word "understanding" comes from the Greek word *nous* and it means "the mind". The mind is the control centre of the soul. Therefore, Paul is again making a clear distinction between the spirit and the soul. Paul again makes a distinction between your spirit, soul and body in Romans 12:1-2:

> *I beseech you therefore, brethren, by the mercies of God, that you present your bodies a living sacrifice, holy, acceptable to God, which is your reasonable service. And do not be conformed to this world, but be transformed by the renewing of your mind, that you may prove what is that good and acceptable and perfect will of God.*
>
> *Romans 12:1-2*

The word "transformed" comes from the Greek word *metamorphoo* and it means "a transformation or change that occurs from the inside out". In 2 Corinthians 4:16, Paul refers to your spirit as the "inward man". The word "inward" comes from the Greek word *esothen* and it means "from inside". Therefore, all three parts of your triune being are found within Romans 12:1-2, in that it communicates the presentation of your body as a living sacrifice and the renewing of your mind (the control centre of the soul), in and through the power of your spirit.

You Are A Complex Triune Being

Let's now take a deeper look at the individual parts of your complex triune being:

Your Spirit

First and foremost, let's expel the myth that your spirit is no more than a mere cloud or bubble on the inside of your belly. Your spirit is not a mere cloud or bubble, your spirit is heavenly person. Ephesians 3:14-16 and Ephesians 4:24 confirm this vital reality:

For this reason I bow my knees to the Father of our Lord Jesus Christ, from whom the whole family in heaven and earth is named, that He would grant you, according to the riches of His glory, to be strengthened with might through His spirit in the inner man.

Ephesians 3:14-16

And that you put on the new man which was created according to God, in true righteousness and holiness.

Ephesians 4:24

Your spirit is the part of you that is created in true righteousness and holiness and the part of you that Paul clearly refers to as the inner man and the new man. Again, not a mere cloud or bubble located somewhere inside your physical body. But a spiritual person, created according to God in true righteousness and holiness. Consider the vital words of Paul contained within 2 Corinthians 5:16-17:

> *Therefore, from now on, we regard no one according to the flesh. Even though we have known Christ according to the flesh, yet now we know him thus no longer. Therefore, if anyone is in Christ, he is a new creation; old things have passed away; behold, all things have become new.*
>
> *2 Corinthians 5:16-17*

Your spirit man is the primary you. God first and foremost knows you according to your spirit man. You are to first and foremost know yourself according to your spirit man. Your spirit man is a new creature, a new species of being. All old things have passed away from your spirit man and your spirit has become new.

Your Soul (Mind, Desires & Emotions)

Your soul is a complex machine made up of differing parts; your mind, your desires and your emotions. Your mind is the control centre of your soul. Your mind and the established mindsets within your mind, determine the direction and order of your desires and emotions, which in turn determine your actions and overall direction in life.

Your desires are internal driving forces designed to move you in a certain direction. What you focus on with your eyes and your imagination, will determine what they drive you to. Focus your eyes and imagination on God's good, acceptable and perfect will and your desires will move you in that direction. Focus your eyes and your imagination on that which is outside of God's good, acceptable and perfect will and your desires will move you in that direction.

Your emotions are feelings on the inside caused by pain or pleasure, that carry the potential to move you in a certain direction. God gave us emotions as a gift that would not only move us towards His good, acceptable and perfect will, but enable us to fully enjoy and experience it in all of its fullness. Negative words and experiences carry the potential to birth negative emotions that can move us away from God's good, acceptable and perfect will. However, praise God, we have the power to govern and bring any negative emotions under control.

The Body

If your soul is a complex machine, then your body is a complex earth-suit. Complex in that it testifies so strongly of our creator God's divine design, with its diversity of cells, parts and functions. Yet it is an earth-suit all the same. Genesis 2:7 confirms this reality:

And the Lord God formed man of the <u>dust</u> of the ground and breathed into his nostrils the breath of life; and man became a living being.

Genesis 2:7

The word "dust" comes from the Hebrew word *aphar* and it means "clay earth, mud and ashes". The word "breathed" comes from the Hebrew word *naphach* and it means "to inflate". The Lord God formed Adam's physical body from the materials and minerals of the ground and He breathed into that body the breath of life and man became a living being. God formed an earth-suit from the materials and minerals of the ground, and He inflated that earth-suit with Adam's spirit and soul.

It has been scientifically proven that the human body is made up of materials and minerals found on the surface of the ground. The most abundant element, oxygen, makes up 65% of the human body; carbon makes up 18% of the human body and hydrogen makes up 10% of the human body. The other 7% is made up with other materials and minerals found on the surface of the ground. All 59 elements within the human body are found on the earth's crust.

Rightly Dividing the Word of Truth

In 2 Timothy 2:15, Paul writes concerning the vital importance of rightly dividing the word of truth.

> *Be <u>diligent</u> to present yourself approved to God, a worker who does not need to be ashamed, rightly <u>dividing</u> the word of truth.*

> *2 Timothy 2:15*

The term 'be diligent' comes from the Greek word *spoudazo* and it speaks of a prompt, earnest and diligent study. The word "dividing" comes from the Greek word *orthotomeo* and it means "to dissect with scalpel-like precision". God's approved method of studying the word of truth is never a shallow surface read, but a precise surgical procedure. A surgical procedure that begins with rightly dissecting yourself as a complex three-part being. Once you have come to understand that you are a three-part being, you can then come to understand the contrasting New Covenant realities concerning your spirit, soul and body. Let's explore some of those contrasting realities together.

Your Spirit Is Fully Regenerated, Your Soul is Being Renewed.

Your Spirit is Fully Regenerated

Consider the revelation of our spiritual regeneration contained within Titus 3:5:

But when the kindness and the love of God our Savior toward man appeared, not by works of righteousness which we have done, but according to His mercy He saved us, through the washing of <u>regeneration</u> and renewing of the Holy Spirit.

Titus 3:4-5

The word "regeneration" comes from the Greek word *paliggenesia* and it means "spiritual rebirth". Here is the glorious truth: if you have confessed with your mouth the Lord Jesus and believed in your heart that God has raised Him from the dead in accordance with Romans 10:9, and if you have called upon the name of the Lord in accordance with Romans 10:13, your spirit has been gloriously rebirthed. This mighty truth is so beautifully complemented by the revelatory flow of 1 Corinthians 6:9-11:

Do you not know that the unrighteous will not inherit the Kingdom of God? Do not be deceived. Neither fornicators, nor idolaters, nor adulterers, nor homosexuals, nor sodomites, nor thieves, nor covetous, nor revilers, nor extortioners will inherit the Kingdom of God. And such were some of you. But you were <u>washed</u>, but you were sanctified, but you were justified in the name of the Lord Jesus and by the Spirit of our God.

1 Corinthians 6:9-11

The word "washed" comes from the Greek word *apolouo* which is made up of the two individual Greek words *apo* and *louo*. The first Greek word *apo* means "to put off or to put away". The second Greek word *louo* means "to bathe fully the whole person". When you confessed with your mouth the Lord Jesus and believed in your heart that God raised Him from the dead, a mighty spiritual force hit your spirit-man; all sin was removed, put away and remitted. Your spirit-man was fully bathed from top to bottom in what Titus 3:5 describes as the washing of regeneration. It is only from this revelatory flow that we can truly understand the much-quoted words of Jesus contained within John 3:1-8;

There was a man of the Pharisees named Nicodemus, a ruler of the Jews. This man came to Jesus by night and said to him, "Rabbi, we know that You are a teacher come from God; for no one can do these signs that You do unless God is with him". Jesus answered and said to him, "Most assuredly, I say to you", unless one is born again, he cannot see the Kingdom of God". Nicodemus said to Him, "How can a man be born when he is old? Can he enter a second time into his mother's womb and be born?" Jesus answered, "Most assuredly, I say to you, unless one is born of water and the Spirit, he cannot enter the Kingdom of God. That which is born of the flesh is flesh, and that which is born of the Spirit is spirit. Do not marvel that I said to you, 'You must be born again'. The wind blows where it wishes, and you hear the sound of it, but cannot tell where it comes from and where it goes. So is everyone who is born of the Spirit."

John 3:1-8

In John 3:7, Jesus boldly declares, "you must be born again." The word "again" comes from the Greek word *anothen* and it means "from above". Therefore, a more accurate translation of John 3:7 would read, "you must be born from above." To be born again is to be born from above; to be born from above is to be begotten again of the Father in accordance with 1 Peter 1:3:

Blessed be the God and Father of our Lord Jesus Christ, who according to His abundant mercy has <u>begotten</u> us again to a living hope through the resurrection of Jesus Christ from the dead.

1 Peter 1:3

The word "begotten" is from the Greek word *anagennao* and it means "to procreate again, to bear again, to conceive again, to birth again". Praise God, your spirit has been born again;

your spirit has been born from above; your spirit has been begotten of God and your spirit has been fully regenerated.

Your Spirit is Fully Regenerated, Your Mind is Being Renewed.

<u>Your Mind is Being Renewed</u>

Consider the words of Paul recorded in Romans 12:2:

> *And do not be conformed to this world, but be transformed by the <u>renewing</u> of your mind, that you may prove what is that good and acceptable and perfect will of God.*
>
> *Romans 12:2*

The word "renewing" comes from the Greek word *anakainosis* and it speaks of a progressive ongoing renovation. It is God's will that your soul is renewed. In other words, your soul should be going through a progressive, day by day, week by week, ongoing renovation. The key to this progressive renovation is a flow of authentic New Covenant repentance (which we will look at in detail in Chapter 4). Let's read Romans 2:4 together:

> *Or do you despise the riches of His goodness, forbearance, and long suffering, not knowing that the goodness of God leads you to <u>repentance</u>?*
>
> *Romans 2:4*

The word "repentance" comes from the Greek word *metanoia* and it means "a change of mind that leads to a change of actions". Notice that authentic New Covenant repentance relates to a change of mind and not a change of spirit. Why? Because your spirit-man has been fully changed, created according to God after true righteousness and holiness. Your spirit is fully regenerated, but your soul is still in the process of being renewed.

Your Spirit is Fully Saved, Your Soul is Being Saved.

Your Spirit is Fully Saved

Consider the words of Paul recorded in Ephesians 2:7-9:

That in the ages to come He might show the exceeding riches of His grace in His kindness toward us in Christ Jesus. For by grace you have been <u>saved</u> through faith, and that not of yourselves; it is the gift of God, not of works, lest anyone should boast.

Ephesians 2:7-9

The word "saved" comes from the Greek word *sozo* and it means "to be rescued or delivered from danger, destruction, sin and sickness". The word "faith" comes from the Greek word *pistis* and it means "to consent". The split second you consented to the finished work of Jesus Christ, that finished work being the new covenant sealed with His blood, your spirit was rescued and delivered from all danger, destruction, sin and sickness. Your blood-bought spirit is the primary you and you are saved.

Your Spirit is Fully Saved, Your Soul is Being Saved.

Your Soul is Being Saved

Consider the words of James 1:21 and Hebrews 10:38

Therefore lay aside all filthiness and overflow of wickedness, and receive with meekness the implanted word, which is able to save your souls.

James 1:21

But we are not of those who draw back to perdition, but of those who believe to the saving of the soul.

Hebrews 10:39

Your spirit is fully saved and your soul is in the process of being saved. James clearly exhorts us to receive the implanted Word, which is able to save our souls. The writer of Hebrews exhorts us to believe to the saving of the soul. Your soul is clearly not yet fully saved. The general terminology used within today's church to describe people coming to faith in Christ is that of "souls being saved". This is biblically incorrect. For the most part, the terms "souls being saved" and "being born again" are used interchangeably within today's church. This again is biblically incorrect. You could say I am splitting theological hairs. However, when it comes to the church maturing and bearing fruit, it is the little foxes that spoil the vine. Consider the weighty words of revelation contained within 1 Peter 1:8-9:

> *Though now you do not see Him, yet believing, you rejoice with joy inexpressible and full of Glory, <u>receiving the end of your faith - the salvation of your souls.</u>*
>
> *1 Peter 1:8-9*

The beginning of your faith is the salvation of your spirit. The end of your faith is the salvation of your soul. The primary word for "change" within the New Testament comes from the Greek word *metamorphoo* and it means "a change that takes place from the inside out". In truth the saving of your soul can only truly begin when your spirit is born again. Your spirit is fully saved, and your soul is being saved, from your fully saved spirit.

Your Spirit is Fully Sanctified, Your Soul is Purified.

<u>Your Spirit is Fully Sanctified</u>

Consider the bold declaration located within Hebrews 10:10:

By that will we have been sanctified through the offering of the body of Jesus Christ once for all.

Hebrews 10:10

The word "sanctified" comes from the Greek word *hagiazo* and it means "to make holy". When you confessed with your mouth the Lord Jesus and believed in your heart that God raised Him from the dead, a mighty spiritual force hit your spirit-man; all sin was removed, put away and remitted. Your spirit-man was fully bathed from top to bottom in what Titus 3:5 describes as the washing of regeneration and your spirit was made holy. Let this strong and concrete truth sink into your heart. Your spirit, the primary you, the part of you that God knows you after, the part of you that you are to know yourself after, is perfectly holy. The following Scriptures, confirm this truth, beginning with 1 Corinthians 1:2;

To the church of God which at Corinth, to <u>those who are sanctified</u> in Christ Jesus, called to be saints, with all who in every place call on the name of Jesus Christ our Lord, both theirs and ours.

1 Corinthians 1:2

And such were some of you. But you were washed, but <u>you were sanctified</u>, but you were justified in the name of the Lord Jesus and by the Spirit of our God.

1 Corinthians 6:11

Jude, a bondservant of Jesus Christ, and brother of James, To those who are called, <u>sanctified by God the Father</u>, and preserved in Jesus Christ.

Jude 1:1

For by one offering He has perfected forever <u>those who are being</u> sanctified.

Hebrews 10:14

The original text of Hebrews 10:14 does not contain the words 'those who are being'. A more accurate translation of Hebrews 10:14, could read as follows.

For by one offering He has perfected and forever sanctified.

Hebrews 10:14 (accurate paraphrase)

The word "forever" comes from the Greek word *dienekes* and it means "perpetually". The word "perpetually" means "continuous, constant, without interruption, continuing forever in the same way". Praise God, by the one once-and-for-all offering of the body of Jesus Christ your spirit is perpetually sanctified. The Passion Translation confirms this explosive truth, in and through its clear and beautiful translation of Hebrews 4:11;

And by his one perfect sacrifice he made us perfectly holy and complete for all time!

Hebrews 4:11 Passion Translation

Your Spirit is Fully Sanctified, Your Soul is Being Purified.

Your Soul is Purified

Consider the exhortation of Peter, located within 1 Peter 1:22:

Since you have <u>purified your souls</u> in obeying the truth through the Spirit in sincere love of the brethren, love one another fervently with a pure heart

1 Peter 1:22

The word "truth" comes from the Greek word *aletheia* and it means "uncovered, unveiled and fully revealed". Authentic New Covenant truth is the unveiling and full revelation of everything that you are and have in the Father. It's the unveiling and full revelation of your fully-regenerated, saved and sanctified spirit. The word "obeying" comes from the Greek word *hupakoe* and it means "an attentive hearing that leads to an active submission, compliance and conformity". Your soul is purified when you hear and actively submit, comply and conform to the truth concerning your fully regenerated, saved and sanctified spirit.

Your Spirit is a Finished Work, Your Soul is a Work in Progress.

Your Spirit is a Finished Work

Consider again the power-packed text, that is 2 Corinthians 5:16-17;

Therefore, from now on, we regard no one according to the flesh. Even though we have known Christ according to the flesh, yet now we know Him thus no longer. Therefore, if anyone is in Christ, he is a new creation; old things have passed away; behold all things have <u>become</u> new.

2 Corinthians 5:16-17

Your spirit-man is in Christ. Your spirit-man is a new creation. Old things have passed away from your spirit-man and all things have become new. The word "become" comes from the Greek word *ginomai* and it means "to be finished". An accurate paraphrase of 2 Corinthians 5:17, would read as follows:

Therefore, if any man is in Christ, he is a new creation; old things have passed away; behold all things have been <u>finished</u> new.

2 Corinthians 5:17 (paraphrase)

Praise God! When you confessed with your mouth the Lord Jesus and believed in your heart that God raised Him from the dead, a mighty spiritual force hit your spirit-man, all sin was removed, put away and remitted. Your spirit-man was fully bathed from top to bottom in what Titus 3:5 describes as the washing of regeneration, your spirit was saved and made holy and finished new. Your spirit, the primary you, the part of you that God knows you after, the part of you that you are to know yourself after, is a finished work. The following Scriptures confirm this truth, beginning with Hebrews 10:14:

> *For by one offering He has <u>perfected</u> forever those who are being sanctified.*
>
> *Hebrews 10:14*

The word "perfected" comes from the Greek word *teleioo* and it means "to complete, to fulfil, to finish". Colossians 2:10 confirms this mighty truth:

> *For in Him dwells all the fullness of the Godhead bodily; and you are <u>complete</u> in Him, who is the head of all principalities and power.*
>
> *Colossians 2:9-10*

Remember you are a spirit, you have a soul and you live in a body. Your spirit is the primary you and you are complete in Him. In and through the once-and-for-all offering of the body of Jesus Christ, your spirit has been completed and is a fully finished work.

Your Spirit is a Finished Work, Your Soul is a Work in Progress.

Your Soul is a Work in Progress

Consider the words of Paul, located within Philippians 1:6:

Being confident of this very thing, that He who has begun a good work in you will complete it until the day of Jesus Christ.

Philippians 1:6

The split second you confessed with your mouth the Lord Jesus and believed in your heart that God has raised Him from the dead, God began a good work in your life and that good work began with the full regeneration and consecration of your spirit. The primary Greek word relating to transformation and change within the New Testament is *metamorphoo* and it means "a transformation/change that occurs from the inside out". Your spirit is a finished work and from that finished work God will finish the ongoing renovation of your soul.

Your Spirit is Fully Regenerated, Your Soul is Being Renewed, Your Body Will be Glorified.

Your Body will be Glorified

Consider informative words that relate to the source and make up of your body, located within Genesis 3:19:

In the sweat of your face you shall eat bread, Till you return to the ground, For out of it you were taken; For dust you are, And to dust you shall return.

Genesis 3:19

Again, Genesis 3:19 is clearly in relation to your physical body. The human body is 100% biodegradable in that it came from the dust of the ground and it will return to the dust of the ground to decompose into the seed of your promised glorified body. The Passion Translation plainly articulates this truth in and through its presentation of 1 Corinthians 15:42-44:

And that's how it will be with the resurrection of the dead. The body is "sown" in decay but will be raised in immortality. It is "sown" in humiliation, but will be raised in glorification. It is "sown" in weakness but will be raised in power. If there is physical body, there is also a spiritual body.

1 Corinthians 15:42-44 Passion Translation

In order to expand upon this, let's read and unpack Philippians 1:21:

For to me, to live is Christ, and to <u>die</u> is gain.

Philippians 1:21

The word "die" comes from the Greek word *apothnesko* and it is the combination of two individual Greek words, *apo* and *thenesko*. The Greek word *apo* means "a separation or a departure". The Greek word *thenesko* means "to decay". Did you know that when a person dies, the human body instantaneously becomes 21 grammes lighter? In other words, at the point of dying, something instantaneously separates and departs from the body, leaving it 21 grammes lighter. Dying is the separation and departure of your spirit and soul from your body, leaving it 21 grammes lighter. The words of Paul, located within 2 Corinthians 5:8 complement this revelatory flow:

We are confident, yes, well pleased rather to be <u>absent</u> from the body and to be <u>present</u> with the Lord.

2 Corinthians 5:8

The word "absent" comes from the Greek word *ekdemeo* and it means "to vacate". The word "present" comes from the Greek word *endemeo* and it means "to be at home". Dying is your spirit and soul vacating your body in order to be at home with the Lord.

Your spirit is your body's primary source of life and whatever is separated from its primary source of life immediately begins to experience *thenesko* (decay). The split second your spirit and soul separate and depart from your body, it begins to experience *thenesko* (decay). Your 100% biodegradable earth-suit begins to decompose and so it is sown back into the earth from which it came, to become the seed of your future glorified body.

Your body may well be a complex earth-suit, with its diversity of cells, parts and functions, however, once it becomes separated from its primary source of life (your spirit), it instantaneously becomes a mass of decomposing clay.

Your Spirit is Fully Regenerated, Your Soul is Being Renewed, Your Body is a Neutral Accommodator.

Your Body is a Neutral Accommodator

Your complex earth-suit is also a neutral accommodator, in that it exists to accommodate the direction and flow of your soul and is 100% neutral about whether that direction and flow is towards God and His good, acceptable and perfect will or otherwise. The Greek word for body is *soma* and it figuratively speaks of a slave, as confirmed in Romans 6:19:

> *I speak in human terms because of the weakness of your flesh. For just as you presented your <u>members as slaves</u> of uncleanness, and of lawlessness leading to more lawlessness, so now present your members as slaves of righteousness for holiness.*
>
> *Romans 6:19*

The word "members" comes from the Greek word *melos* and it means "a limb or a part of the body". Your body is a neutral slave, in that it exists to facilitate the direction and flow of your soul, whatever that direction and flow might be.

Your Spirit is Fully Regenerated, Your Soul is Being Renewed, Your Body Can be in Health.

Your Body can be in Health

Consider the powerful words located within 3 John 2 that articulate God's passionate desire for His beloved Sons and Daughters to be in physical health:

Beloved, I pray that you may prosper in all things and be in health, just as your soul prospers.

3 John 2

The word "health" comes from the Greek word *hugiano* and it means "to have sound health, to be well in your body". It is clearly God's will for your body to be in health in order that you may be well enough to experience all His awesome plans and purposes for you upon the earth.

Notice, that according to 3 John 2, your body will be in health, just as your soul prospers, as confirmed in Romans 12:2:

And do not be conformed to this world, but be transformed by the renewing of your mind, that you may prove what is that good and acceptable and perfect will of God.

Romans 12:2

Again, the word "renewing" comes from the Greek word *anakainosis* and it speaks of a progressive ongoing renovation. The word "transformed" comes from the Greek word *metamorphoo* and it speaks of transformation/change from the inside out. The health of your body is determined by the prosperous renovation of your soul. The prosperous renovation of your soul takes place from your fully regenerated inward man.

In Conclusion, it is God's will that your soul (mind, desires & emotions) be renovated, but your soul is not yet fully born of God. It is God's will that your body be in health, but your body is not yet fully born of God. It is your inward man, your spirit, that is 100% born of God and all authentic New Covenant transformation begins with the revelation of your regenerated, born-of-God spirit. The exhortation of Paul located within Ephesians 4:24, reveals the divine nature and character of your regenerated spirit;

And that you put on the new man which was created according to God,
in true righteousness and holiness.

Ephesians 4:24

What a powerfully radical truth! Your spirit, the part of you that God knows you after and that you are to know yourself after is created according to God, in true righteousness and holiness. The word "new" comes from the Greek word *kainos*, and one of its primary meanings is "regenerated", which again means spiritual rebirth. Your spirit, and only your spirit, is 100% born of God. 2 Peter 1:4 expands upon this key foundational truth:

By which have been given to us exceedingly great and precious promises, that through these you may be partakers of the divine <u>nature</u>, having escaped the corruption that is in the world through lust.

2 Peter 1:4

The word "nature" comes from the Greek word *phusis* and is taken from the Greek word *phuo* which means "to produce, to bring forth, to give birth to". God the Father has given birth to you by the Holy Spirit, to be His Sons and Daughters, as confirmed in 1 Peter 1:23:

Having been born again, not of corruptible <u>seed</u> but incorruptible, through the word of God which lives and abides forever.

1 Peter 1:23

The word "seed" comes from the Greek word *spora* and it means "a sowing" i.e. by implication, parentage; seed. We are Sons and Daughters of divine parentage and God the Father has imparted His very DNA and nature to us, His children. Romans 8:15 supports this truth:

For you did not receive the spirit of bondage again to fear, but you received the Spirit of <u>adoption</u> by whom we cry out, "Abba, Father".

Romans 8:15

The word "adoption" comes from the Greek word *huiothesia* and it means "to be placed as Sons and Daughters within a family". Your spirit is the primary you and you have been born from above, you have been re-birthed from the Father, placed as Sons and Daughters into the family of God and from that Spirit of adoption, we cry "Abba, Daddy". You are born again. You are regenerated, and you are born of God. Romans 8:29 adds even more weight to this flow of New Covenant truth:

For whom He foreknew, He also predestined to be conformed to the image of His Son, that He might be the firstborn among many brethren.

Romans 8:29

The word "firstborn" comes from the Greek word *protokos* and it means "the firstborn of all or the firstborn of many". Jesus through His death, burial and resurrection became the firstborn of many. The firstborn of many what? The firstborn of many Sons and Daughters. We are the "many", as so wonderfully proclaimed in Hebrews 2:10:

For it was fitting for Him, for whom are all things and by whom are all things, in bringing many sons to glory, to make the captain of their salvation perfect through sufferings.

Hebrews 2:10

You don't have to sing about being "a saint that is in that number" any more. You are a saint and you are in that number. Praise God, Jesus is the firstborn of many and we are the many. You may not be the second born, or the third born, or the fourth born. But you are born again, you are born of the Spirit, you are born of God and you are in that number. Now, read Romans 8:29 from the Passion Translation and rejoice in the glorious revelation of everything that you are and have, as the Sons and Daughters of God:

For he knew all about us before we were born and destined us from the beginning to share the likeness of his Son. This means the Son is the oldest among a vast family of brothers and sisters who will become just like Him.

Romans 8:29 Passion Translation

Again, before moving into Chapters 2 & 3, it was vitally important that we first laid the foundational revelation of your spiritual regeneration. If you have confessed with your mouth the Lord Jesus and believed in your heart that God raised Him from the dead in accordance with Romans 10:9 and if you have called upon the name of the Lord in accordance with Romans 10:13, your spirit has been rebirthed and is now 100% born of God. Your spirit, and only your spirit is 100% born of God. This vital revelation is the essential foundational launching pad into the revelations of your forgiveness and justification in Him. Let's now go on to discover these explosive revelations together, beginning with chapter 2 and the powerful New Covenant reality that… You Are Forgiven!

———————————————

In Him we have redemption through His Blood, the forgiveness of sins according to the riches of His Grace.

Ephesians 1:7

———————————————

CHAPTER 2

You are Forgiven

I truly believe that much of the body of Christ has a limited revelation of their forgiveness in Him. I also believe that the revelation of our forgiveness in Him is one of the most explosive revelations of our New Covenant. A revelation that when grasped in its fullness has the power to activate dynamic change in every area of our lives. If you have confessed with your mouth the Lord Jesus and believed in your heart that God has raised Him from the dead in accordance with Romans 10:9, you are born of God and you have received the forgiveness of sins. However, do you fully know what that means? Do you fully know what took place when you consented to the mighty work of forgiveness in your life?

The following Scriptures proclaim our forgiveness in Christ:

In Him we have redemption through His Blood, the forgiveness of sins according to the riches of His Grace.

Ephesians 1:7

And be kind to one and other tender-hearted forgiving one and other even as God has forgiven you.

Ephesians 4:32

He has delivered us from the power of darkness and conveyed us into the Kingdom of the Son of His love in whom we have redemption through His blood the forgiveness of sins.

Colossians 1:14

And you being dead in your trespasses and uncircumcision of your flesh He has made alive together with Him having forgiven you all trespasses.

Colossians 2:13

I write to you little children because your sins are forgiven you for His name sake.

1 John 2:12

The limited view of your forgiveness is that it brought about a great change in heaven in that the legal record against you was changed from guilty to innocent. That is a powerful revelation, but it is a limited one. You see the primary change that your forgiveness brought about did not take place in heaven but in you.

The work of forgiveness is not just the changing of a heavenly record but the changing of a person. Again, your forgiveness did not just change a legal record in heaven, it changed you and it changed you forever! The word "forgiveness" comes from the Greek word *aphiemi* and it means "to take away, to hurl away, to put away, to disregard, to remit". *Aphiemi* comes from the Greek word *apo* which means "a separation, or a departure unto cessation". In other words, the forgiveness of sin is the sending away of all sin from you, separating you from it forever. Let's take a deeper look at the two elements of forgiveness based on the Greek word *aphiemi*. Firstly, it's a taking away, secondly, it's a separation unto cessation.

The Taking Away

Let's begin to unpack this glorious taking away by looking at John 1:29:

The next day John saw Jesus coming toward him and he said 'Behold the Lamb of God who <u>takes away</u> the sin of the world.

John 1:29

Praise God! Jesus did not come to simply cover our sins, but to take them away. This is clearly confirmed in Hebrews 9:26:

He then would have had to suffer often since the foundation of the world; but now once at the end of the ages He has appeared to <u>put away</u> sin by the sacrifice of Himself.

Hebrews 9:26

The words of Paul contained within 1 Corinthians 6:9-11 build upon this vital revelation:

Do you not know that the unrighteous will not inherit the Kingdom of God? Do not be deceived. Neither fornicators, nor idolaters, nor adulators, nor homosexuals, nor sodomites, nor thieves, nor covetous, nor drunkards, nor reviles, nor extortioners will inherit the Kingdom of God. And such were some of you. But you were <u>washed</u>, but you were sanctified, but you were justified in the Name of the Lord Jesus and by the Spirit of our God.

1 Corinthians 6:9-11

The word "washed" is the Greek word *apolouo* which is made up of the two individual Greek words *apo* and *louo*. The first Greek word *apo* means "to put off or to put away". The second Greek word *louo* means "to bathe fully the whole person". When you confessed with your mouth the Lord Jesus and believed in your heart that God raised Him from the dead, a mighty spiritual force hit your spirit-man, all sin was removed, put away and remitted. Your spirit-man was fully bathed from top to bottom in what Titus 3:5 describes as the washing of regeneration (spiritual rebirth). That force was, the force of forgiveness, the force of *aphiemi.*

The Separation unto Cessation

Again, the first element of forgiveness based on the Greek word *aphiemi,* represents a taking-away. The second element represents a separation unto cessation.

The word "cessation" means "to end, to bring to a termination, a stoppage, a closure". In other words, your forgiveness brought about a separation from sin which in turn brought an end to your connection with sin. In order to gain more insight into the nature of this cessation, let's begin with the words of Paul, contained within Romans 4:7-8:

> *Blessed are those whose lawless deeds are forgiven and whose sins are covered; Blessed is the man to whom the Lord shall not impute sin.*
>
> *Roman 4:7-8*

The words "shall not" come from the Greek words *ou me* and together they mean "never ever, under any circumstance". The word "impute" comes from the Greek word *logizomai* which means "to take inventory or to take account of". In other words, Romans 4:8 literally reads as "Blessed is the man to whom the Lord shall never ever under any circumstance, take inventory or take account of his sin".

As a born-again believer and as the righteousness of God in Christ Jesus, God will never ever, under any circumstance, take inventory (keep a record of) or keep an account of sin in your life. Why? Because He chooses to turn a blind eye to it and pretend it never happened? No! Is it because God has a selective memory and he has chosen to forget about it or blank it out of his mind? Again, no! So then, why does God not take inventory or keep an account of any sin in your life? Are you ready for the answer? Now don't close the book and throw it in the bin. Stay with this, read on and let the Spirit of God liberate you into true and lasting freedom from sin.

Why does God never ever under any circumstance take inventory or keep an account of sin in your life? The answer … because you didn't do it! What! I know that's a massive statement. But don't close up on it now, let's dig into it, beginning with 2 Corinthians 5:16-17:

Therefore, from now on we regard no one according to the flesh even though we have known Christ according to the flesh yet now we know him thus no longer. Therefore, if any man be in Christ he is a new creation, old things have passed away behold all things have become new.

2 Corinthians 5:16 - 17

God does not know you after the flesh but after your recreated, born of God, fully washed spirit-man. He knows you after the primary you which is your inward man, your spirit-man. With this in mind let's read 1 John 3:9.

Whoever has been <u>born of God</u> does not sin for His seed remains in him and he <u>cannot</u> sin, because he has been born of God.

1 John 3:9

The word "cannot" comes from the Greek words *ou me* which as we have seen already mean "never ever, under any circumstance". So according to 1 John 3:9, whoever is born of God can never ever under any circumstance sin. Which part of you is born of God? Your spirit-man is born of God. The part of you that God knows you after, the part of you that you are to know yourself after, is born of God and whoever is born of God can never ever, under any circumstance, sin. Now you can see why it was so vital to establish the foundational revelation of your born of God (born again) spirit, in chapter 1. The split second you became a born-again child of God your spirit-man lost any leaning or ability to sin. Again, the word "forgiveness" comes from the Greek word *aphiemi*. *Aphiemi* means "to send away, to hurl away, to put away, to disregard, to remit". *Aphiemi* comes from the Greek word *apo*, which means "a separation unto cessation".

Your sins are forgiven, past, present and future, not because God took away your past sins and chose to turn a blind eye to your present and future sins. Your sins are forgiven; past, present and future, because God took away your past sins and recreated your spirit-man. In recreating your spirit-man, God took away your spirit-man's ability to sin, either in the present or the future. Boom! That's New Covenant forgiveness in all of its radical glory. Your born-again recreated spirit has no ability to reconnect with sin. And since your spirit-man is the primary you, you cannot sin, you have not sinned, and you will not sin again!

You may say "But I have sinned as a born-again child of God and I continue to sin as a born-again child of God". Not with your spirit you haven't, and with your spirit you don't and with your spirit you won't! It's with your soul and your body that you sin. Your spirit-man does not participate in any way because, again, whoever is born of God cannot participate in sin. This is why repentance, which is the Greek word *metanoia* means "a change of mind which leads to a change of actions". Not a change of spirit. It's why your spirit-man is "saved" according to Ephesians 2:8 and your soul is "being saved" according to James 1:21. It's why your spirit-man is "washed" once and for all according to Titus 3: 5 and your soul is "being washed" continuously according to Ephesians 5:26. It's why your spirit-man is recreated in "righteousness and true holiness" according to Ephesians 4:24 and your soul is being "renewed" according to Romans 12:2.

Reflect on the statements that you have just read and awaken again to the reality that we will never learn to rightly divide the word of truth according to 2 Timothy 2: 15 until we learn to rightly divide our three-part being according to 1 Thessalonians 5:23. Your spirit-man, the primary you, the part of you that God knows you after and the part of you that you are to know yourself after, has experienced a radical and eternal transformation in and through the powerful force that is forgiveness (*aphiemi*). Again, *aphiemi* means "to send away, to hurl away, to put away, to disregard, to remit" and comes from the Greek word *apo*, which means "a separation unto cessation". All sin has been removed from your born of God recreated spirit and your born of God recreated spirit is forever separated and forever finished with sin.

Is this not the ultimate licence to sin? That is a vital question. If you are truly preaching the gospel of Jesus Christ, you will birth this question. If you are truly preaching the Gospel of Jesus Christ, you, like Paul, will be required to answer this question. If your Gospel does not birth this question, it's at best a limited version of The Gospel and at worst, another Gospel. Let's begin to answer this vital question, by reading the words of Paul, in Titus 2:11-12:

For the grace of God that brings salvation has appeared to all men teaching us that, denying ungodliness and worldly lusts we should live soberly righteously and godly and the present age.

Titus 2:11-12

This revelation of New Covenant forgiveness may be radical, but it is not a licence to sin. This is the grace of God that brings salvation and teaches us how to deny ungodliness and worldly lusts that we may live soberly, righteously and godly in this present age. This revelation of forgiveness carries the potential to activate an authentic and consistent flow of godliness and holiness that religious Christianity has only ever sung and preached about, but never, if truth be told, consistently walked in. Remember that the word "forgiveness" derives from the Greek word *apo* meaning a separation or a departure unto cessation. With this in mind, let's consider Romans 6:1-2:

What shall we say then? Shall we continue in sin that grace may abound? Certainly not! How shall we who died to sin live any longer in it?

Romans 6:1-2

"How shall we who died to sin live any longer in it?" Which part of you died to sin and as a result is finished with it? It's the part of you that is born of God, your spirit-man, the primary you. Romans 6:6 adds even more weight to this vital flow of revelation:

Knowing this that are old man was crucified with him, that the body of sin might be done away with, that we should no longer be slaves to sin.

Romans 6:6

Paul starts off by saying, "knowing this". Knowing what? Knowing that our old man was crucified with him, that the body of sin might be done away with. The term "done away with" comes from the Greek word katargeo which means "to abolish, to destroy, to bring to naught". Paul is telling us that our old man was crucified with Him and in being crucified with Him, it was abolished, destroyed and brought to naught. What old man? Your old spirit-man was crucified with Him, your old sinful nature has been abolished, destroyed and brought to naught, in and through the powerful force of forgiveness. Both Romans 6:7 and Romans 6:11 confirm this magnificent truth:

For he who has died, has been freed from sin.

Romans 6:7

Likewise, you, also reckon yourself to be dead indeed to sin, but alive to God in Christ Jesus.

Romans 6:11

Grace is not, "Well we all sin, we all miss it, after all we are only human, but thank God His grace covers our sin!" Grace did not come to cover our humanity, grace came to overwhelm our humanity, with the power and life of heaven.

A limited revelation of grace starts with the premise that we are only human. However, an authentic revelation of grace starts with the premise that we are not only human, we are in fact spirit-beings. And if you are a spirit-being that has consented to the finished the work of Jesus Christ, you are a spirit-being that is made in the likeness and image of God. Righteous, holy, forgiven, separated and finished with sin. In other words, you have the potential as a born-again child of God to live completely free from sin. Remember from chapter 1 of this book that we are the begotten of God. Did the First Begotten sin, even when He faced the same temptations as we face on this earth? No! Then the second begotten and the third begotten and whatever number you are in the glorious New Covenant genealogy, have the potential not to sin. Yes, but aren't we all only human? In order to answer that question, let's unpack Paul's rebuke to the believers at Corinth, contained within 1 Corinthians 3:3:

For are you still carnal for where there are envy strife and divisions among you are you not carnal and behaving like <u>mere men</u>?

1 Corinthians 3:3

The term "mere men" comes from the Greek word *anthropos*, which means "a human being". Listen to what Paul literally says in 1 Corinthians 3:3, "Are you not carnal and acting like mere human beings?" How could Paul say such a thing?

Because he knows that as Sons and Daughters of God we are not simply mere human beings. We are spirit-beings, created in the image and likeness of God, righteous, holy, pure, forgiven, dead to sin and addicted to His good, acceptable and perfect will.

Walking in The Spirit

Consider Paul's strong declaration contained within Galatians 5:16:

Walk in the spirit and you <u>shall not</u> fulfil the lust of the flesh.

Galatians 5:16

Remember that we discovered that the term "shall not" comes from the Greek words *ou me* and it means "never ever under any circumstance". Listen to what Paul literally says in Galatians 5:16, "Walk in the spirit and you shall never ever under any circumstance, fulfil the lust of the flesh or you could say sin". Why? Because your born of God, recreated spirit can never ever under any circumstance, reconnect with sin. Wow! What a radical declaration. This is the immeasurable potential of our regenerated, born of God spirit. This is the true potential of the Sons and Daughters of God. This is the divine fruit of our radical New Covenant forgiveness. This is the grace of God that brings salvation and teaches us how to deny ungodliness and worldly lusts that we may live soberly, righteously and godly in this present age. This is our calling and our pre-ordained destiny.

Has any child of God, outside of Jesus, ever walked in the fullness of what Paul refers to in Ephesians 4:24, as "the new man". Have I personally been taught by grace to the point that I am walking in this life, completely free from sin? No, I have not. However, that does not mean that I cannot, and it does not change the reality that as a born-again child of God, I have the potential to do so.

It's at this stage of my writing that I sit back in my chair and I question. I don't question what I have written as I believe it to be New Covenant truth. I don't question that my spirit-man, the primary me, is forgiven to the point that it has not and will not ever sin. I don't question the reality that my spirit-man is dead to sin and alive to God. I don't question the reality that if I or any other born-again believer truly walked in the life and power of our regenerated spirit, that we will not in any way fulfil the lust of the flesh. I don't even question the reality of my potential to live a sin free life, just as my perfect example Jesus did. All these things I am convinced to be the truth. What I do question is this: am I a fool to even consider that I or any of my brothers and sisters reading this book could live a life completely free from sin? Is this no more than a doctrinal ideal that is simply unattainable in this far-from ideal world? And yet as I pause and as I doubt, I hear the Spirit of God speak to my heart,

"Craig you're asking the wrong questions. Don't ask "Has anyone outside of Jesus ever walked this earth completely free from sin?". Don't even ask if you or anyone else reading this book could ever come to or attain that place of freedom. Ask Me only about the damage you could do to the kingdom of darkness upon the way. Ask Me about the glory that will arise upon you, upon the way. Ask Me about the days of heaven on earth you will experience, upon the way. Ask Me about the harvest that will come to your light, upon the way. Don't try to reason this out, just start walking. Walk with Me and work with Me, watch how I do it. Learn the unforced rhythms of grace. Walk in the Spirit and together we will make a mark upon this earth that cannot be erased."

The mighty force of *aphiemi* has blasted all sin from your born of God recreated spirit and your born of God recreated spirit is forever separated and finished with sin. Who Are You? You Are Forgiven! My prayer concerning "Who are You?" is that it would help launch you into a flow of authentic New Covenant repentance. However, before we move towards that in chapter 4, we must first put in place the second part of the launch pad. The first part of the launch pad was the revelation of your forgiveness. The second part of that launch pad is the revelation of your justification. Let's move into chapter 3 together and study the powerful revelation that 'You Are Justified'!

Therefore, having been justified by faith we have peace with God through our Lord Jesus Christ.

Romans 5:1

CHAPTER 3

You are Justified

The word "justified" comes from the Greek word *dikaioo* and it means "to render innocent, a divine acquittal and pardon". If you have confessed with your mouth the Lord Jesus and believed in your heart that God has raised Him from the dead in accordance with Romans 10: 9, you are born of God and you are justified. The following Scriptures proclaim our justification In Christ:

Therefore, having been justified by faith we have peace with God through our Lord Jesus Christ.

Romans 5:1

Moreover, whom He has predestined these He also called, whom He called these He also justified and whom He justified, these He also glorified.

Romans 8:30

That having been justified by His grace we should become heirs according to the hope of eternal life.

Titus 3: 7

You have been acquitted, you have been pardoned and you are innocent. In order to fully grasp and come to understand this revelation of your justification and of your divine acquittal, pardon and innocence, we must first review the mighty force of forgiveness.

Again, as we studied in Chapter 2, the limited view of your forgiveness is that it brought about a great change in heaven and that the legal record against your life was changed from guilty to innocent. However, as I have stated, the primary change that forgiveness brought about did not take place in heaven, but in you. The work of forgiveness is not just the changing of a heavenly record, but the changing of a person. Your forgiveness did not just change a legal record in heaven, it changed you and changed you forever!

And now as a result of the transformational work of forgiveness, you are justified; acquitted, pardoned and innocent. You see, the limited view of forgiveness presents it as a divine pardon which would make your forgiveness and your justification one and the same. However, they are not one and the same; they are two distinct revelations. Forgiveness is the divine force that birthed your justification, or you could say that forgiveness was the divine action that resulted in your justification.

Let's review the revelation of forgiveness and if needs be, take time to personally reflect upon Chapter 2. Remember: this is not a book to be simply read but a collection of revelations to be studied and meditated upon. The word "forgiveness" comes from the Greek word *aphiemi* and it means "to take away, to disregard, to remit". *Aphiemi* comes from the Greek word *apo*, which means "a separation or a departure unto a cessation". In other words, the forgiveness of sin is the sending away of all sin from you, separating you from it forever. When you confessed with your mouth the Lord Jesus and believed in your heart that God raised him from the dead, a mighty spiritual force hit your spirit-man, all sin was removed, put away and remitted. Your spirit-man was fully bathed from top to bottom, in what Titus 3:5 describes as the washing of regeneration. In other words, your spirit-man was born of God. Let's look again at 1 John 3:9;

Whoever has been born of God does not sin, for His seed remains in him and he <u>cannot</u> sin, because he has been born of God.

1 John 3:9

Again, the word "cannot" comes from the Greek term *ou me* which means "never ever, under any circumstance". So according to the 1 John 3:9, whoever is born of God, can never ever, under any circumstance sin. Which part of you is born of God? Your spirit-man is born of God! The part of you that God knows you after, the part of you that you are to know yourself after, is born of God and whoever is born of God can never ever, under any circumstance sin. The split second you were born again your spirit-man lost any leaning or ability to sin. Your sins are forgiven, past present and future, not because God took away your past sins and chose to turn a blind eye to your present and future sins. Your sins are forgiven, past present and future, because God took away your sins and recreated your spirit-man. And in recreating your spirit-man, God took away your spirit-man's ability to sin, either in the present or in the future. Your born again, recreated spirit has no ability to reconnect with sin.

Now since your spirit-man is the primary you, you cannot sin, you have not sinned, and you will not ever sin again. But you may say "But I have sinned as a born-again child of God and I continue to sin as a born-again Child of God". Not with your spirit you haven't and with your spirit you don't and with your spirit you won't! It is with your soul and body that you sin. Which again is why repentance (which we will study in the next chapter) comes from the Greek word *metanoia* which means "a change of mind that leads to a change of actions"; not a change of spirit. It is a new creation reality that when you sin your spirit-man does not participate in any way! Your spirit, in partnership with the Holy Spirit, will correct and challenge when you sin. But in no way will your spirit-man participate, because again whoever is born of God cannot under any circumstance sin. This is why you are justified. This is why you are eternally acquitted. This is why you are eternally pardoned, and this is why you are eternally innocent. Consider these words written by Paul to the church at Corinth.

Open your heart to us. We have <u>wronged</u> no man, we have corrupted no one, we have cheated no one.

2 Corinthians 7:2

The word "wronged" comes from the Greek word *adikeo* and it means "to do an injustice, to act criminally or unrighteously, to violate any human or divine law, to do wrong, to mistreat others". *Adikeo* consists of being guilty, of general wrongdoing, and inflicting hurt or damage on individuals. What Paul is literally saying in 2 Corinthians 7:2, is that he has done no wrong and he has not damaged or hurt any individuals. In other words, when it comes to doing any wrong, especially concerning damaging or hurting any individuals, Paul declares himself not guilty and completely innocent. But wait a minute, is this not the same Paul who empowered the violent and at times murderous persecution of the early church? Is this not the same Paul who consented to the execution of Stephen? The answer is no, it's not the same Paul. The man Paul is referring to in 2 Corinthians 7:2

has truly wronged no man, is truly not guilty and is truly innocent. The man responsible for so much of the bloody persecution of the early church, died on the road to Damascus. The man that Paul is referring to in 2 Corinthians 7:2 is the new man, the regenerated man, the forgiven man, the born of God man, and the fully and eternally justified man. And just like Paul, you and I, as the Sons and Daughters of God, can boldly declare that we have done no wrong, we are not guilty, we are innocent, and we are justified.

It is so vitally important that we seize the revelation of our justification. Let's study the exhortation of Peter, in 1 Peter 5:8:

Be sober, be vigilant; because your adversary the <u>devil</u> walks about like a roaring lion, seeking whom he may devour.

1 Peter 5:8

The word "devil" comes from the Greek word *diablous* and it means "a slanderer and a false accuser". In connection with this, the Hebrew word for "satan" is *sawtan* and it means "to attack with accusation". The Greek word for "satan" is *satanas* and it means "the accuser". The word "adversary" in 1 Peter 5:8 comes from the Greek word *antidikos* and it means "a court room opponent".

The Spirit of God, through Peter, exhorts us to be sober and vigilant. Why? Be sober, be vigilant, because your court room opponent walks about roaring false accusations, seeking to devour you with guilt. Guilt is an illegal cancer that has absolutely no business within the body of Christ. The justified Sons and Daughters of God should have no connection whatsoever with guilt. We are not the guilty; we are the acquitted, the pardoned, the innocent. Guilt must be totally resisted, and our adversary overcome. How do we overcome him? The answer to this vital question is located within Revelation 12:9-11:

So, the great dragon was cast out, that serpent of old, called the devil and Satan, who deceives the whole world; he was cast to the earth, and his angels were cast out with him. Then I heard a loud voice saying in heaven, 'Now salvation and strength, and the Kingdom of our God, and the power of His Christ have come, for the accuser of our brethren who accused them before our God day and night, has been cast down. And they overcame him by the blood of the Lamb and the word of their testimony, and they did not love their lives onto death.

Revelation 12:9-11

We overcome him by the blood of the Lamb and the word of our testimony. We overcome the accuser by the revelation of the blood of the Lamb. The very core of this triumphant revelation is clearly communicated in the following Scriptures;

The next day John saw Jesus coming towards him, and said, "Behold the Lamb of God who takes away the sin of the world!

John 1:29

In whom we have redemption through His blood, the forgiveness of sins.

Colossians 1:14

In Him we have redemption through His blood, the forgiveness of sins according to the riches of His grace.

Ephesians 1:7

We overcome the accuser by the revelation that through the precious blood of Christ, a lamb without blemish or spot, we are forgiven. Your spirit-man, the primary you, the part of you that God knows you after and the part of you that you are to know yourself after, has experienced a radical and eternal transformation in and through the powerful force that is forgiveness. All sin has been removed from your born of God recreated spirit and your born of God recreated spirit is forever separated and finished with sin. And since your spirit-man is the primary you, you cannot sin, you have not sinned, and you will not sin again! This is why you are eternally innocent. This is why you are forever justified. And this is why you can overcome the accuser with one strong and perfect plea and one bold and concrete testimony. We plead the blood and boldly declare that we have received a divine acquittal, that we have received an eternal pardon and that we are forever innocent!

So, who are you? You are born of God. You are forgiven. You are justified. Again, on the outer court of every vital New Covenant truth there are erroneous extremes. My prayer concerning "Who are you?" is that the spirit of God would use it to take you past the outer courts of erroneous extremes and into the inner courts of authentic New Covenant truth. That you would truly grasp the truth of your spiritual rebirth in Him, that you would truly grasp the truth of your forgiveness in Him and that you would truly grasp the truth of your justification in Him. I believe that when truly grasped and understood, these radical truths will not bring you to a place of passivity and self-indulgence which may well be the fruit of the erroneous outer court extremes. However, the fruit of authentic inner court truth is explosive and lasting change. An explosive and lasting change that can only come into being through the dynamic force of authentic New Covenant repentance. An authentic repentance that is rooted, grounded and empowered in and from the place of innocence. Let's move forward into the next phase of "Who are you?"; Chapter 4: Repentance from the place of innocence.

Let us therefore come boldly to the throne of grace, that we may obtain mercy and find grace to help in time of need.

Hebrews 4:16

CHAPTER 4

Repentance from the place of innocence

S in is the ultimate form of self-harm, in that it brings about an immediate, but temporary relief from pressure yet leaves long-term damaging wounds in your life. The Father God is passionate about seeing His Sons and Daughters free from sin with its harmful and damaging wounds. When you sin as a Son or Daughter of God you sin with your soul and your body but not your spirit-man. Remember that according to 1 John 3:9 whoever is born of God can never ever under any circumstance sin. Which part of you is born of God? Your spirit-man is born of God. The part of you that God knows you after, the part of you that you are to know your self after, is born of God and whoever is born of God can never ever under any circumstance sin. The split second you became a born-again child of God, your spirit-man lost any leaning or ability to sin. So again, when you sin as a Son or Daughter of God you sin with your soul and body and not your spirit.

Your soul is your mind, your desires and emotions. The mindsets or the strongholds of your mind determine the direction and order of your desires and emotions. Therefore, you could say that when you sin as a child of God you sin with your mind and body. A more practical way of putting it would be that you sin with your mind and actions. Which is why the term "repentance" in the New Testament comes from the Greek word *metanoia* and it means "a change of mind that leads to a change of actions".

The primary Greek word for sin within the New Testament is *hamartia* and is mentioned 174 times. The secondary Greek word for sin is *hamartano* and is mentioned only 48 times. The primary Greek word for sin, *hamartia,* is a noun that describes the primary source of wrong actions; that primary source being the mind. The secondary Greek word for sin, *hamartano,* is a verb which describes the wrong actions that flow from the source of wrong thinking. In other words, *hamartia* (wrong thinking) precedes *hamartano* (wrong actions). Sin is first and foremost *hamartia* (wrong thinking) that leads to *hamartano* (wrong actions) which can only be eliminated by a powerful flow of *metanoia* (a change of mind that leads to a change of actions).

Be sober, be vigilant; because your adversary the <u>devil</u> walks about like a roaring lion, seeking whom he may devour.

1 Peter 5:8

As we learned in chapter 3, the word "devil" comes from the Greek word *diabolos* and it means "a slanderer and false accuser". In connection with this the Hebrew word for "satan" is *sawtan* and it means "to attack with accusation". The Greek word for "satan" is *satanos* and it means "the accuser". The word "adversary" in 1 Peter 5:8 comes from the Greek word *antikos* and it means "a court room opponent". When you sin as a Son or Daughter of God, Satan, your accuser, wants to bring you to the courtroom, to stand in guilt. When you sin as a child of God, the Spirit of God wants to bring you to the throne room to sit in your innocence. Consider the powerful invitation, that is Hebrews 4:16:

Let us therefore come boldly to the throne of grace, that we may obtain mercy and find grace to help in time of need.

Hebrews 4:16

We are to come boldly to the throne of God. What are we to do upon our arrival at the throne of Grace? The answer is found in Ephesians 2:6:

And raised us up together, and made us sit together in the heavenly places in Christ Jesus.

Ephesians 2:6

So, what are we to do upon our arrival at the throne of Grace? We are to sit down with our big Brother (Jesus) next to our Daddy (God). Then from that family seat, we place the practices and habits of self-harm on the table and open our soul to the warmth of home that is the warm empowerment of His Grace. The Father God, by His Spirit, wants to teach us to sit in our innocence with Him, and from that seat of innocence we place the sin that is still in our minds and actions on the table. Together we formulate a plan to deal with it once and for all.

When you stand in the place of guilt you address sin from a place of insecurity, inferiority and inevitable defeat. When you sit in the seat of innocence you address sin from a place of security, superiority and inevitable victory. Be in no doubt, authentic New Covenant repentance from the place of innocence can and will bring about explosive and lasting change in every area of your life. Let's look at the biblical example of New Covenant repentance from the place of innocence and the dynamic fruit it bears in the lives of God's Sons and Daughters.

During Paul's three-year ministry in Ephesus on his third missionary journey he received disturbing reports concerning sin among the believers at Corinth. This eventually resulted in him writing a corrective letter that we now know as 1 Corinthians. We will also look at one of Paul's follow-up letters that we now know as 2 Corinthians. Let's look at some of the sin issues that Paul addressed in his corrective letter to the believers at Corinth.

In 1 Corinthians 1:10-17 Paul addresses the sin of sectarianism. The believers at Corinth were gathering around individual leaders within the church and forming divisive sects resulting in strife and contention throughout the local body.

In 1 Corinthians 6:12-20, Paul also addresses the sin of fornication. The word "fornication" comes from the Greek word *porneia* and it means "every and any form of illicit sexual activity", i.e. sexual activity outside of the covenant of marriage between a man and a woman.

In 1 Corinthians 11:17-34 Paul confronts the sins of gluttony and drunkenness around the Lord's table. In other words, the believers at Corinth were arriving at the Lord's supper in their own individual divisive sects devouring all the food and drink for themselves, without even the slightest consideration for their brothers and sisters throughout the local body. Without even mentioning some of the other issues Paul addressed in and through 1 Corinthians we have established a clear picture of the sin that existed within this local body. And yet let's investigate a little further.

As already mentioned, in 1 Corinthians 1:10-17 Paul addresses the sin of sectarianism with the church at Corinth. Now, let's unpack what Paul says in the following verse that is addressing this very sin issue.

> *Now I say this, that <u>each of you</u> says, "I am of Paul," or "" am of Apollos," or "I am of Cephas," or "I am of Christ".*
>
> *1 Corinthians 1:12*

The term "each of you" comes from the same Greek word *hekastos* and it means "each and every one", or you could say "every single person within the collective whole". Listen to what Paul is literally saying in 1 Corinthians 1:12:

> *Now I say this that each and every single one of you says, "I am of Paul," or "I am of Apollos," or "I am of Cephas," or "I am of Christ".*
>
> *1 Corinthians 1:12 (paraphrase)*

Therefore, it is accurate to say that each and every single believer within the Corinthian church was practicing the sin of sectarianism. Not every believer within the Corinthian church was practicing the sin of fornication. Not every believer within the Corinthian church was practicing the sin of gluttony and drunkenness around the Lord's table. However, every believer within the Corinthian church was practicing the sin of sectarianism and therefore every believer within the Corinthian church was practicing sin. With this in mind, let us look at how Paul begins the corrective letter of 1 Corinthians, keeping in mind that every believer within the Corinthian church was practicing sin.

Paul, called to be an apostle of Jesus Christ through the will of God, and Sosthenes our brother, To the church of God which is at Corinth, to those who are sanctified in Christ Jesus, called to be saints, with all who in every place call on the name of Jesus Christ our Lord, both their and ours.

1 Corinthians 1:1-2

First let's observe Paul's words in verse 2:

To the church of God, which is at Corinth, <u>to those who are sanctified</u> in Christ Jesus.

Notice that it does not say, "to those who are being sanctified". In fact, the words "to those who are" are not in the original text. The original text of 1 Corinthians 1:2 reads as follows:

To the church of God, which is at Corinth, <u>sanctified</u> in Christ Jesus.

1 Corinthians 1:2 (paraphrase)

The word "sanctified" comes from the Greek word *hagiazo* and it means "to be made holy, purified and consecrated". Now let's read 1 Corinthians 1:1-2 from the Passion Translation:

From Paul, divinely appointed according to the plan of God, to be an apostle of the Anointed One, Jesus. Our fellow believer Sosthenes joins me in writing you this letter addressed to the community of God throughout the city of Corinth. For you have been made pure, set apart in the Anointed One, Jesus...

1 Corinthians 1:1-2 (Passion Translation)

Paul clearly addresses the church in Corinth as those who have been sanctified, as those who have been made holy, as those who have been purified and consecrated in Christ Jesus. How can Paul address the church at Corinth as sanctified when each and every believer is practicing sin? Paul was simply practicing what he preached in 2 Corinthians 5:16-17:

Therefore, from now on, we regard no one according to the flesh. Even though we have known Christ according to the flesh, yet now we know Him thus no longer.

2 Corinthians 5:16

What was Paul doing in addressing the church at Corinth as sanctified when each and every one of them was practicing sin? Paul wasn't knowing them according to the flesh, but according to the spirit. Paul was first and foremost choosing to know them after the part of them that was 100% sanctified and not the part of them that was still being sanctified i.e. their soul.

Paul, first and foremost, addresses the believers at Corinth according to their 100% sanctified spirits and not according to their sin. Paul does not address them according to their right spirit in order to ignore their wrong thinking *(hamartia)* which was driving their wrong actions *(hamartano)*. Remember: sin is the ultimate form of self- harm that leaves long-term harmful and damaging wounds. Paul, like his Commander-in-Chief is passionate about seeing his brothers and sisters free from all cycles of self-harm, that damage and wound their lives. Paul's ultimate goal is to bring them to authentic repentance, to bring them to *metanoia*, a change of mind that leads to a change of actions. Let's give thought to the words of Paul contained within Romans 12:1-2:

I beseech you therefore, brethren, by the mercies of God, that you may present your bodies a living sacrifice, holy, acceptable to God, which is your reasonable service. And do not be conformed to this world, but be

*<u>transformed</u> by the <u>renewing</u> of your mind, that you may prove what is
that good and acceptable and perfect will of God.*

Romans 12:1-2

The word "transformed" comes from the Greek word
metamorphoo and it means "to fashion or change from the
inside out". *Metamorphoo* is the primary New Testament word
for change. This is because all authentic New Covenant
change flows from the inside out. The word "renewing" in
Romans 12:2 comes from the Greek word *anakainosis* and it
means to "renovate".

With all of this in mind, consider the cycle of authentic New
Covenant transformation and change. You could call it "the
methamorphoo cycle". The key to walking free from sin and
consistently walking in the good acceptable and perfect will
of God is the renovation of the mind. The key to the
renovation of the mind, is authentic New Covenant
repentance, *metanoia,* a change of mind that leads to a change
of actions. Authentic New Covenant repentance flows from
the inside out. Authentic New Covenant transformation
begins with who you are inside; it begins with your inward
man. The call to authentic New Covenant transformation is a
call to be who you already are.

Before Paul spoke to the Corinthian believers about the sin that they were practicing, he spoke to them about who they were. Before Paul spoke to them about their wrongdoing, he spoke to them about their right-being. Paul first and foremost addresses them as born of God, forgiven, justified, sanctified, set apart, holy Sons and Daughters of God. In so doing Paul shut down Satan's primary plan to take them to his courtroom to stand in guilt and activated the Father's plan to bring them into His throne room to sit in their innocence. It is then from that place of innocence that a forceful flow of authentic New Covenant repentance was activated, which brought about the manifestation of authentic New Covenant transformation and change. This forceful flow and its fruit are recorded in 2 Corinthians 7:8-11. Let's study it together.

For even if I made you sorry with my letter, I do not regret it; though I did regret it. For I perceive that the same epistle made you sorry, though only for a while. Now I rejoice, not that you were made sorry, but that your sorrow lead to repentance. For you were made sorry in a godly manner, that you might suffer loss from us in nothing. For godly sorrow produces repentance leading to salvation, not to be regretted; but the sorrow of the world produces death. For observe this very thing, that you sorrowed in a godly manner: What diligence it produced in you, what clearing of yourselves, what indignation, what fear, what vehement desire, what zeal, what vindication! In all things you proved yourselves to be clear in this matter.

2 Corinthians 7:8-11

Let's take a closer look at the potent individual fruit produced by a flow of authentic New Covenant repentance.

Godly Sorrow

For godly sorrow produces repentance leading to salvation, not to be regretted; but the sorrow of the world produces death.

2 Corinthians 7:10

Born-again believers who practice a religious form of repentance are most often masters of apology and yet amateurs of change. Religious repentance is centred around a limited, guilt-driven apology. A guilt-driven apology that acts as a form of emotional penance, that brings about a limited shift in the emotions but little to no change of mind or actions. Making the front of the church sanctuary an altar of emotional penance for guilt-ridden believers may make for a so-called good meeting; it will not, however, make for strong Sons and Daughters of God overcoming sin in and through an authentic change of mind and actions. Should we, as Sons and Daughters of God, be sorry when we sin? Absolutely, yes! However, not with a worldly sorrow that is fuelled by guilt and produces a fruitless form of emotional penance. But with a Godly sorrow that is fuelled by His goodness and produces authentic fruit bearing repentance.

What then is the make-up of this Godly sorrow? I believe that it first and foremost consists of being sorry that we have grieved God. In other words, the Godly sorrow that we should experience when we sin begins with the reality that we have grieved God. Religious repentance begins with a sorrow that is fuelled by guilt and is related to the anger of God. However, the grieving that God experiences when His Sons and Daughters sin is not a grieving that is compatible with His anger but with His lovingkindness. Observe the covenant declaration contained within the 63rd Psalm:

Because Your <u>loving kindness</u> is better than life, My lips shall praise You.

Psalm 63:3

The word "lovingkindness" comes from the Hebrew word *checed.* The word *checed* is mentioned 248 times in the Old Testament and 139 times by David in the Psalms. David was a man after God's own heart because God's heart is a heart of *checed. Checed* is the heart force of Heaven. *Checed* is the DNA of Eden, the DNA of the Abrahamic covenant and the DNA of our glorious New Covenant. *Checed* is God's obsessive, aggressive, relentless commitment to the divine well-being of all humanity. A divine well-being that must be consented to, but a divine well-being that is towards all humanity, nonetheless. Let's bring this home to land for you personally. *Checed* is God's obsessive, aggressive, relentless, commitment to you and your divine well-being. Let's consider Matthew 10:30:

> *But the very hairs of your head are all <u>numbered</u>.*
>
> *Matthew 10:30*

The word "numbered" comes from the Greek word *arithmeo* and it means "counted". I truly love my wife Tracey, but I have never laid awake at night and counted the number of hairs on her head! Think about it, God has counted the very hairs on your head, that's *checed! Psalm 17:8 articulates God's glorious heart of checed:;*

> <u>*Keep*</u> *me as the apple of your eye; Hide me under the shadow of Your wings.*
>
> *Psalm 17:8*

The word "keep" comes from the Hebrew word *shamar* and it means "to constantly watch over and observe". God is constantly watching over you as the apple of His eye. That's *checed!*

Remember sin is the ultimate form of self-harm, in that it brings about an immediate, but temporary relief from pressure yet leaves long-term harmful and damaging wounds.

What does this self-harming do to our heavenly Daddy, a heavenly Daddy who has a relentless heart of *checed* towards us? It grieves Him. We grieve God when we sin because we hurt ourselves and it grieves the *checed* heart of the Father to see his children damaged and wounded.

If godly sorrow first and foremost consists of being sorry that we have grieved God when we sin, then I believe that it secondly consists of being sorry that we have been neglecting and missing out on the superior goodness of God. Sin is not only the ultimate form of self-harm, sin is an active submission to inferior sources of satisfaction, fulfilment and comfort. Inferior sources that are outside of God's good, acceptable and perfect will for every area of your life. Consider the following Scriptures that articulate the nature of God's will:

And do not be conformed to this world, but be transformed by the renewing of the mind, that you may prove what is that good and acceptable and perfect will of God.

Romans 12:2

For it is God who works in you both to will and to do for His good pleasure.

Philippians 2:13

As His divine power has given us all things that pertain to life and godliness, through the knowledge of Him who called us by glory and virtue.

2 Peter 1:3

Authentic New Covenant repentance begins with an awakening to God's good, acceptable and perfect will for every area of our lives. It begins with an awakening to the reality of His good pleasure. It begins with the reality that He has already given to us all things that pertain to His *zoe* (the Greek word for the God kind of life) life and godliness. Through this awakening, and this awakening alone, comes a godly sorrow concerning our foolish neglect of the superior goodness of God. Romans 2:4 confirms the vital importance of this awakening to God's goodness:

Or do you despise the riches of His goodness, forbearance, and longsuffering, not knowing that the goodness of God leads you to repentance?

Romans 2:4

The word "goodness" comes from the Greek word *chrestos* and it simply means "better". I love the powerful simplicity of this. It's the better of God that leads to repentance. It's the better of God that leads us away from all inferior sources of satisfaction, fulfilment and comfort. It's the better of God that brings about a godly sorrow. A godly sorrow that we have been neglecting and missing out on the superior goodness of God.

In reflection, godly sorrow first and foremost consists of being sorry that we have grieved God. Secondly, godly sorrow consists of being sorry that we have been neglecting and missing out on the superior goodness of God. Thirdly, I believe that godly sorrow consists of being sorry for a short and limited amount of time. Let's read 2 Corinthians 7:8 together:

For even if I made you sorry with my letter, I do not regret it; though I did regret it. For I perceive that the same epistle made you sorry, though only for a while.

2 Corinthians 7:8

The term "only for a while" comes from the Greek word *hora* and it means "an instant, an hour, a day" and it carries the connotation of a short and limited amount of time. We should be sorry that we sin as Sons and Daughters of God. We should be sorry that we have grieved God by harming and wounding ourselves. We should be sorry that we have been neglecting and missing out on the superior goodness of God. However, we should only be sorry for a limited and short amount of time.

Consider this; when driving your car, first gear is the right and appropriate gear in which to start your journey. In other words, you start to move off in first gear. However, it's only the right and appropriate gear for a short and limited amount of time. If you do not quickly and efficiently move through the other gears, first gear will go from being your beneficial starting point, to your detrimental point of breakdown. To put it in more simple terms, if you stay too long in first gear, you might burn out your clutch, your car will start smoking and ultimately it will breakdown. Godly sorrow is the first gear of authentic repentance, godly sorrow is the right and appropriate gear for getting you moving in your journey of authentic repentance. However, if you stay too long in godly sorrow it will evolve into guilt, your soul will begin to experience religious burnout and your journey of authentic repentance and authentic change will breakdown. Remember: the primary fuel of religious repentance is guilt, which drives you to practice a form of emotional penance.

One of the first signs that you have stayed in first gear for too long whilst driving a car is the smell of smoke. One of the first signs that you have stayed in godly sorrow for too long is that you start to let off the smoke of emotional penance. An emotional penance that can come accompanied with sincere tears. An emotional penance that can come with the ideal worship song playing the in background. An emotional penance that can come to you on your knees at the altar of a church sanctuary. An emotional penance that looks and sounds extremely pious and yet in the eyes and nostrils of God it's no more than a form of religious smoke and a sure-fire sign that your soul is experiencing religious burnout.

So again, should we be sorry that we sin? Should we experience the first gear of authentic repentance that is godly sorrow? Absolutely, yes! However, only for a short and limited amount of time. A mature and equipped driver recognises the necessity to start in first gear but goes on to quickly and effectively move through the other gears; and the quicker the better. Let's now move from the first gear of godly sorrow through the other gears of authentic New Covenant repentance.

Diligence

For observe this very thing, that you sorrowed in a godly manner: What diligence it produced in you...

2 Corinthians 7:11

The word "diligence" comes from the Greek word *spoude* and it means "speed, eagerness, forwardness and haste". When you sit in your innocence and allow God to awaken you to His superior goodness, a glorious haste is activated within your spirit-man. As you continue to feed on His goodness and soak in His presence, that haste floods into your soul causing you to move away from the sin that has been so easily ensnaring you at record-breaking speed. The flow of authentic New Covenant repentance flows from your spirit at record-breaking speed bringing about a record-breaking change in your mind and actions. A dynamic change that is well beyond the realms of religious Christianity. Who says change must take a long time? Admittedly, change can be a long, drawn-out process for a mere human being changing in and through their own human strength and ability; however, we as the Sons and Daughters of God are not mere human beings. Let's look again at Paul's challenge to the believers at Corinth contained within 1 Corinthians 3:3:

For you are still carnal. For where there are envy, strife, and divisions among you, are you not carnal and behaving like <u>mere men</u>?

1 Corinthians 3:3

The term "mere men" comes from the Greek word *anthropos* and it simply means "human beings". Paul is quite literally correcting the saints at Corinth for behaving and walking out this life as mere human beings. We, as the Sons and Daughters of God are not mere human beings. The same spiritual momentum that raised Jesus from the dead lives within us! And when activated appropriately it will quickly and effectively drive every sin and weakness out of our lives. As the spiritual Sons and Daughters of God, our journey of change is perpetual in that we should always be changing. However, because we are the spiritual Sons and Daughters of God, the individual phases of being changed from glory to glory do not have to be prolonged and drawn-out. In fact, the quicker we power away from the sin that so easily ensnares, the quicker we get to pour all of our spiritual energies into seeing the kingdoms of this world become the Kingdom of our Lord, and the earth being filled with the knowledge of the glory of the Lord as the waters cover the sea. When it comes to authentic New Covenant repentance, when it comes to the changing of your mind that leads to a changing of actions, when it comes to powering away from the sin that can so easily ensnare you, the acceleration of Heaven is within you and You Are SPEED!

Clearing of yourselves

˙ For observe this very thing, that you sorrowed in a godly manner: What diligence it produced in you, what <u>clearing of yourselves</u>…

2 Corinthians 7:11

The term "clearing of yourselves" comes from the Greek word *apologia* and it means "an honest, straight-forward plea and apology that is free from excuse and self-defence". Consider the powerful Kingdom declaration contained within Romans 5:17:

For if by one man's offence death reigned through the one, much more those who receive abundance of grace and of the gift of righteousness will reign in life through the One, Jesus Christ.

Romans 5:17

As the Sons and Daughters of God we are called to rule and reign in life. One of the most vital aspects of that rule and reign is our rule and reign over sin. How do we rule and reign over sin? By receiving abundance of grace. How do we receive abundance of grace? The answer is found in Hebrews 4:16:

Let us therefore come boldly to the throne of grace, that we obtain mercy and find grace to help in time of need.

Hebrews 4:16

We receive the grace to rule and reign over sin by coming boldly to the throne of grace. What do we do upon our arrival at the throne of grace? We sit down in accordance with Ephesians 2:6:

And [He] raised us up together, and made us sit together in the heavenly places in Christ Jesus.

Ephesians 2:6

Upon our arrival at the throne of grace we sit down. We sit down in our innocence with our big brother and next to our Daddy. From that family seat we place the practices and habits of self-harm on the table in an open and honest manner. An open and honest manner that is free from any form of excuse or self-defence. One of the primary fruits of self-righteousness is self-defence. Self-righteousness can often produce the fruit of self-defence because the self-righteous see Jesus as their courtroom prosecutor rather than their throne room intercessor and advocate. The self-righteous will often defend their wrong actions as if their eternal life and destiny depended on it, because in their mind, and only in their mind, it does. We are not the self-righteous, we are the righteousness of God in Christ Jesus. We are not the accused, we are the innocent. We do not stand as the accused, we sit as the innocent without any sense of guilt and inferiority.

We no longer foolishly try to hide from God when we sin because we know that He sees us as innocent. We no longer hide sin because the hiding place of sin is the breeding place of guilt and we as the Sons and Daughters of God have no business with guilt, and no business hiding sin. As the righteousness of God in Christ Jesus, as the forgiven, justified Sons and Daughters of God, we come boldly to the throne of grace. We sit in our innocence, we place any sin that is still in our minds and actions on the table in an open, honest manner. No more pretence, no more hiding, no more excuses, no more self-defence. Just a beautifully vulnerable clearing of ourselves, in order to receive His amazing grace, His wisdom, His plan and His ability to rule and reign over all sin.

Indignation

For observe this very thing, that you sorrowed in a godly manner: What diligence it produced in you, what clearing of yourselves, what indignation…

2 Corinthians 7:11

The word "indignation" comes from the Greek word, *aganaktesis* and it means "to be moved with anger". According to 2 Corinthians 7:11 there is a godly indignation and anger that is a vital ingredient of authentic New Covenant repentance. A godly indignation and anger that moves us away from sin and towards His good pleasure. Observe the exhortation of 1 Peter 5:8:

Be sober, be vigilant; because your adversary the devil walks about like a roaring lion, seeking whom he may devour.

1 Peter 5:8

The Spirit of God through Peter exhorts us to be sober and vigilant. Why? Be sober, be vigilant because your adversary the devil seeks to make you your own worst enemy. If satan can get you to believe the lie that God is angry with you, it will cause you to cower away from God and in turn become angry at yourself. When you become angry at yourself you begin to self-assassinate and quite literally, become your own worst enemy. You begin to attack and assassinate your worth, your value, your right-standing with God and your free access to His grace.

We are not the guilty, we are the justified. We do not stand as the guilty before an angry God. We sit as the innocent, fully-accepted and at ease in the beloved. As we sit in our innocence with Him, a godly indignation and anger begins to arise from within our spirit. Not an anger that is fuelled by guilt and that leads to self-assassination, but an anger that is fuelled by grace and leads to the assassination of sin. An anger that has quite frankly had enough of the self-harming that wounds and damages. An anger that attacks any sin that still ensnares us with the Kingdom weaponry of faith, hope and love. An anger that moves us into the good, acceptable and perfect will of God.

Fear

For observe this very thing, that you sorrowed in a godly manner: What diligence it produced in you, what clearing of yourselves, what indignation, <u>what fear</u>...

2 Corinthians 7:11

The word "fear" comes from the Greek word, *phobos* and it means "to be alarmed, frightened, to be afraid". According to 2 Corinthians 7:11 there is a fear that is a vital ingredient of authentic New Covenant repentance. As New Covenant Sons and Daughters of God we are to be afraid of something, but what? Are we to be afraid of God? In order to answer this vital question, let's begin by again reading Hebrews 4:16:

Let us therefore come boldly to the throne of grace, that we may obtain mercy and find grace in time of need.

Hebrews 4:16

The word "boldly" comes from the Greek word *parrhesia* and it means "an outspoken confident assurance". The word "come" comes from the Greek word *proserchomai* and it means "to approach". As the Sons and Daughters of God we are to approach His throne with an outspoken, confident assurance.

The primary basis for this confident and assured approach is located within Hebrews 11:6:

But without faith it is impossible to please Him, for he who comes to God must believe that He is, and that He is a rewarder of those who diligently seek Him.

Hebrews 11:6

The primary basis for approaching God with a confident assurance is believing that He is, for he who approaches God must believe that He is... that He is what? 1 John 4:16 tells us what He is:

And we have known and believed the love that God has for us. <u>God is love,</u> and he who abides in love abides in God, and God in him.

1 John 4:16

The primary basis for approaching God with a confident assurance is believing that God is love. God does not have love, He is love. Now, because God is love we can boldly say in line with 1 Corinthians 13:4-8, that God is longsuffering, God is kind, God does not envy, God does not parade Himself, God is not puffed up, God does not behave rudely, does not seek His own, is not provoked, thinks no evil, does not rejoice in iniquity but rejoices in truth; bears all things, believes all things, hopes all things, endures all things. God never fails. We are to approach God with a confident assurance that He is all these things, and that these are the things He has for us. Is there anything in that glorious list that we should possibly be afraid of? Absolutely not! Should we as the Sons and Daughters of God be in any way afraid of love Himself? No way! But, we should according to 2 Corinthians 7:11 be afraid of something when it comes to being in a flow of authentic repentance. So again, what is it? Is it the judgement of God that we should be afraid of? In order to answer this crucial question, let's begin by reading 1 John 4:17:

Love has been perfected among us in this: that we may have boldness in the day of judgment; because as He is, so are we in this world.

1 John 4:17

We, as the beloved Sons and Daughters of love should in no way be afraid of judgement. Love has been perfected among us in this, that we may have a confident assurance in the day of judgement because as He is (and He is Love) so are we in this world. So, if it's not God whom we are to be afraid of and it's not the judgement of God that we are to be afraid of when it comes to being in a flow of authentic repentance, what is it? Let's dig a little deeper, beginning with Philippians 2:12-13:

Therefore, my beloved, as you have always obeyed, not as in my presence only, but now much more in my absence, work out your own <u>salvation</u> <u>with</u> fear and trembling; for it is God who works in you both to will and to do for His good pleasure.

Philippians 2:12-13

The word "salvation" comes from the Greek word *soteria* and it means "deliverance, preservation, soundness, prosperity, health, happiness, rescue and overall well-being". The word 'with' in verse 12 comes from the Greek word *meta* and it means "an immediate accompaniment". An accompaniment is a complementary attachment. Paul in Philippians 2:12 exhorts us as the Sons and Daughters of God to work out our own salvation with the complementary attachments of fear and trembling. Work out the deliverance, the preservation, the soundness, the prosperity, the health, the happiness, and the overall well-being that is yours in Christ Jesus, with the complementary attachments of fear and trembling. Consider Romans 8:16-17:

The Spirit Himself bears witness with our spirit that we are children of God, and if children, then heirs - heirs of God and joint heirs with Christ, if indeed we suffer with Him, that we may also be glorified together.

Romans 8:16-17

What is an heir? An heir is an individual who receives ownership of an allotted inheritance. As the children of God, we are joint owners with Christ and owners of salvation. All of the powerful fruits of *soteria* mentioned above are ours, as joint heirs with Christ. This is why Paul tells us in Philippians

2:12 to work out our <u>own</u> salvation *(soteria)*. As owners of *soteria* work it out with fear and trembling. Work out your own *soteria* with the complementary attachments of fear and trembling. How can fear be a complementary attachment to *soteria?* Are you to be afraid of preservation, soundness, prosperity, health, happiness and overall well-being? Absolutely not! You should most definitely not fear any part of *soteria*. You should, however, fear it not being worked out into every area of your life for one plain and simple reason, it is way too good to miss out on!! Consider Ephesians 1:13:

In Him you also trusted, after you heard the word of truth, <u>the gospel of your salvation</u>; in whom also, having believed, you were sealed with the Holy Spirit of promise.

Ephesians 1:13

The word "gospel" comes from the Greek word *euaggelion* and it means "the almost too-good-to-be-true news". The almost too-good-to-be-true news of our salvation, is that it is way too good to miss out on. It's the *soteria* of God, not just for your spirit, but for your soul, your body, your marriage, your children, your finances and for every single area of your life. Therefore you do not want to miss out on any part of it, because it's exceedingly abundantly above all you could ask or think! Hebrews 4:1 adds even more strength to this glorious flow of revelation:

Therefore, since a promise remains of entering His <u>rest</u>, let us fear lest any of you seem to have come short of it.

Hebrews 4:1

The word "rest" in Hebrews 4:1 comes from the Greek word *katapauo* and it means "to colonise". Your spirit is a complete and perfect colony of heaven. Now, from that heavenly colony God wants to partner with you in the colonisation of your soul, your body, your marriage, your children, your finances, your family, your community, your city. In fact, this flow of Kingdom colonisation does not end until the kingdoms of the world have become the Kingdom of our Lord and the earth is filled with the glory of the Lord as the waters cover the seas. Therefore, since the promise remains of entering into a life fully colonised in the Eden grace of God; therefore, since the promise remains of entering into a life fully colonised in the *soteria* of heaven, let us fear lest any of us seem to have come short of it. Let us fear lest any of us seem to miss out on any of it.

Some of the most precious memories of my childhood growing up in Belfast revolve around my Granny Martin's house. Almost every week night, my Mother, Aunts, Uncles and my Granny and Grandad would all come together in my Granny Martin's living room to play a board game called

Ludo. The room was truly alive with lots of noise, lots of humour and laughter and quite a few arguments! I remember as kids we absolutely loved being there on these special nights. We as kids may have loved it but the adults, especially my Granny disliked us being what she described as, "under their feet." The question of why we as kids wanted to sit in with them when we could have been out playing with our friends was constantly put to us throughout the night. My Granny Martin's answer to this question was straight and to the point. "You kids are afraid of missing something!" Granny Martin also had a specific term she would use to describe us kids staying in her house when we could have been outside playing with our friends. She called it "clocking", which meant to hang around in a specific place. I can almost hear her shouting at us now, "What are you kids doing clocking in here all night when you could be out playing with your friends? You are all afraid of missing something!" She was right, we truly were afraid of missing something. For instance, I can remember a bomb exploding just down the road from Granny Martin's house. So close, in fact, that the whole house shook. Usually when something like that happened the local community would come out of their houses and congregate at the scene of what had just happened. However, not even a bomb going off was enough to move us out of Granny Martin's living room. Why? Because as kids we were truly afraid of missing something.

We as the children of God have been invited to walk in His good acceptable and perfect will. We have been invited to taste of His goodness and *checed* for every area of our lives and to work out our *soteria* for every area of our lives. And we most definitely need to be afraid of missing out on that! We should be determined to "clock" in His word and "clock" in His presence until every area of our life is colonised in the life and blessing of heaven. This is the fear that is a vital ingredient of authentic New Covenant repentance. This is a fear that comes as a complementary attachment of salvation. This is what we are to be afraid of as the children of God. Not God Himself, not His judgement, but afraid that we will miss out on experiencing any aspect of His unmerited, unearned goodness for every area of our lives. When you truly taste and experience His goodness it will cause you to reverence and honour Him more and more. When you truly taste and experience His goodness it will cause you to tremble in awestruck wonder under the weight of His *checed*. When you truly taste and experience His goodness it will cause you to "clock" in His presence refusing to be moved because you are just too afraid of missing something.

Vehement Desire

For observe this very thing, that you sorrowed in a godly manner: What diligence it produced in you, what clearing of yourselves, what indignation, what fear, what vehement desire...

2 Corinthians 7:11

The term "vehement desire" comes from the Greek word *epipothesis* and it means "an earnest longing for". The word "vehement" in the English dictionary means "forceful, passionate and intense". According to 2 Corinthians 7:11 there is a forceful, passionate and intense longing for that is a vital ingredient of authentic New Covenant repentance. A longing for what, exactly? A longing for the goodness of God. A longing for the good, acceptable and perfect will of God. A longing for His *soteria* made manifest in every area of our lives.

Zeal

For observe this very thing, that you sorrowed in a godly manner: What diligence it produced in you, what clearing of yourselves, what indignation, what fear, what vehement desire, what zeal...

2 Corinthians 7:11

The word "zeal" comes from the Greek word *zelos* and it means "a heated ardour". The definition of "ardour" is "great enthusiasm or passion". Synonyms of ardour are fervour, zeal, eagerness, intensity, zest, gusto, energy, animation, fire. According to 2 Corinthians 7:11 there is a burning red-hot zeal that is a vital ingredient of authentic New Covenant repentance. What is this burning red hot zeal? It is quite simply PURPOSE ON FIRE!

It is the God-ordained purpose for your life, set on fire and burning with a strong and fervent flame! Observe the powerful words relating to the fire of personal purpose contained within 1 Timothy 1:6 of the Passion Translation:

I'm writing to encourage you to fan into a flame and rekindle the fire of the spiritual gift God imparted to you when I laid my hands upon you.

2 Timothy 1:6 (Passion Translation)

One of the most powerful fruits of authentic New Covenant repentance is the fanning into flame and rekindling of the fire of your divine purpose. And what is the best and most effective way to fan into flame and rekindle any fire? Wind! The best and most effective way to rekindle any fire is to employ the appropriate flow of wind. Consider Zechariah 4:6:

'Not by might, not by power, but by My Spirit,' says the Lord of Hosts.

Zechariah 4:6

The word "might" comes from the Hebrew word *chayil* and it means "an army, a band of men, a company, strength in numbers". The word "power" comes from the Hebrew word *koach* and it means "individual strength and ability". The word "Spirit" comes from the Hebrew word *ruwach* and it means "wind". Again, one of the most powerful fruits of the authentic New Covenant repentance is the fanning into flame and rekindling of your divine purpose. Authentic New Covenant repentance can only truly flow from the place of innocence. In other words, the rekindling of your divine purpose can only truly happen from the seat of innocence. It can only truly happen when you sit in the place of your innocence and allow God to blow on your divine purpose.

The sad reality is, that some Christians, especially leaders in the modern-day church system have become strangers to His heavenly wind. This is a wind that can only blow on the seated. Sadly, some Christians within the modern-day church system are too busy building up their numerical strength and their individual strength to take their seat. The corrective reforming shout of heaven for such a time as this, is that it is not by numerical strength or individual strength, but by His wind. No seat, no wind; no wind, no fire; no fire, no authentic kingdom purpose upon the earth. All creation is crying out for the manifestation of the Sons and Daughters of God, and because all creation is crying out for the manifestation of the Sons and Daughters of God, all of heaven is crying out for a seated reformation of wind and fire. Let's be that reformation in Jesus' Name!

<u>Vindication</u>

For observe this very thing, that you sorrowed in a godly manner: What diligence it produced in you, what clearing of yourselves, what indignation, what fear, what vehement desire, what zeal, <u>what vindication</u>...

2 Corinthians 7:11

The word "vindication" comes from the Greek word *ekdikesis* and it means "retribution, revenge and punishment". It quite literally means "to retaliate and hit back". According to 2 Corinthians 7:11 there is a retaliation and revenge attack that is a vital ingredient of authentic New Covenant repentance. What is this retaliation and revenge attack? This attack is not primarily against sin but against the source of the deceit that births sin. This attack is not primarily against religion but against the source of the lies that birth religion. This last and powerful fruit of authentic New Covenant repentance, this vindication, is an attack against the deceiver, against the liar, against the thief that comes to steal, kill and destroy. It is against the devil himself.

This retaliation and revenge attack against the devil is about "cleaning his clock", which is Belfast for "fixing his wagon", which is Belfast for "knocking him into the back of next week", which is Belfast for "giving him a good seeing to", all of which is plain and simple English for giving him a jolly good beating. In order to unpack the make-up of this retaliation and revenge attack, let's begin by considering 2 Corinthians 10:4-6:

For the weapons of our <u>warfare</u> are not carnal but mighty in God for pulling down strongholds, casting down arguments and every high thing that exalts itself against the knowledge of God, bringing every thought into captivity to the obedience of Christ, and being ready to punish all disobedience when your obedience is fulfilled.

2 Corinthians 10:4-6

The word "warfare" comes from the Greek word *strateia* and it means "military service" i.e. (figuratively) the apostolic career. The Greek word *strateia* comes from the Greek word *strateuomai* and it means "to serve in a military campaign, to complete an assigned tour of duty, to execute the apostolate or apostolic mission". In other words, the warfare that Paul writes about in 2 Corinthians 10:4 and indeed the warfare that Paul writes about in 1 Timothy 1:18, entails the carrying out and execution of an assigned apostolic tour of duty. According to Paul, every believer has a primary apostolic tour of duty. Or you could say an apostolic assignment to establish the Kingdom of God in a certain region or place. What is the primary region of your apostolic tour of duty? For the answer to this question, let's unpack 2 Corinthians 10:4:

For the weapons of our warfare are not carnal but mighty in God for pulling down <u>strongholds</u>,

2 Corinthians 10:4

The word "strongholds" comes from the Greek word *ochuroma* and it means "a fortified place of safety, a fortress, a castle and (figuratively) an argument". In biblical times strongholds were commonplace and essential for survival. These strongholds were typically on high ground above a city. When a city would come under attack its rulers and inhabitants would retreat to the city's stronghold for two main reasons. Firstly, they retreated to their stronghold for refuge and safety. Secondly, they retreated to their stronghold in order to formulate the appropriate response to the attack.

Whilst on a mission trip to Greece I visited what remains of the ancient city of Corinth. The highlight for me was not in seeing the ruins of Corinth itself, but in seeing its stronghold, otherwise known as Acrocorinth, set on a hill high above the city. A stronghold that would have been in place in some form during the time of Paul's writing to the church at Corinth. And so, Paul was using the geographical landscape of their city to awaken them to the negative strongholds within their minds, strongholds that needed to be pulled down and abolished. Paul was awakening them to the reality that just as their city had a fortified stronghold of retreat and response, they also had strongholds of retreat and response within their minds. The true biblical definition of a stronghold is not a demon in the sky, but a wrong set way of thinking that exists between people's ears. A stronghold is a mindset that determines your actions in a time of pressure. Let's study 2 Corinthians 10:4-5:

> *For the weapons of our warfare are not carnal but mighty in God for pulling down strongholds, casting down <u>arguments</u> and every high thing that exalts itself against the knowledge of God, bringing every <u>thought</u> into captivity to the obedience of Christ,*
>
> *2 Corinthians 10:4-5*

The word "argument" comes from the Greek word *logismos* and it means "mental reasoning and logical thinking" and it carries the connotation of negative strongholds of limited natural thinking. The word "thought" comes from the Greek word *noema* and it means "perceptions, purposes, dispositions and thoughts within the mind". Let's begin to put this altogether in a practical flow. According to Paul, every born-again child of God has a warfare in which they are called to engage. That warfare is their primary apostolic tour of duty. The primary region of this apostolic tour of duty is the mind. The assigned mission of this apostolic tour of duty is the pulling down of strongholds. The strongholds in question are wrong set ways of thinking that determine our actions in a time of pressure. In other words, they are fortresses of wrong thinking that lead to wrong actions. How then do we pull down these negative strongholds within the mind? Let's unpack 2 Corinthians 10:5:

Casting down arguments and every high thing that exalts itself against the knowledge of God, bringing every thought into captivity to the <u>obedience of Christ,</u>

2 Corinthians 10:5

We are to pull down these negative strongholds by taking every thought captive and subservient to the obedience of Christ. Notice that it does not say "bringing every thought into captivity to our <u>own</u> personal obedience." It clearly says that we are to first and foremost bring every thought into the captivity of the obedience of Christ. What does the obedience of Christ look like? The answer is found in Hebrews 5:8:

Though He was a son, yet He learned obedience by the things that he suffered.

Hebrews 5:8

The obedience of Christ was the suffering of Christ. A suffering that is harrowingly articulated in Isaiah 53:3-5:

He is despised and rejected by men, a Man of sorrows and acquainted with grief. And we hid, as it were, our faces from Him; He was despised, and we did not esteem Him. Surely, He has borne our griefs, and carried our sorrows; yet we esteemed Him stricken, smitten by God, and afflicted. But He was wounded for our transgressions, He was bruised for our iniquities; the chastisement for our peace was upon Him, and by His stripes we are healed.

Isaiah 53:3-5

The obedience of Christ was the suffering of Christ. The obedience of Christ was His death, burial and resurrection. The obedience of Christ is His finished work. The obedience of Christ is our blood-bought forgiveness, our blood-bought justification, our blood-bought righteousness, our blood-bought peace, our blood-bought protection, provision and destiny. The obedience of Christ is our blood-bought victory. When we bring every thought into captivity to our blood-bought victory we are positioned to truly retaliate and activate a devastating revenge attack against the devil. Let's consider 2 Corinthians 10:5-6:

Casting down arguments and every high thing that exalts itself against the knowledge of God, bringing every thought into captivity to the obedience of Christ and being ready to <u>punish</u> all disobedience when your obedience is fulfilled.

2 Corinthians 10:5-6

The word "punish" comes from the Greek word *ekidikeo* and it means "to retaliate, a revenge attack". We retaliate and carry out our revenge attack against the devil when our obedience is fulfilled. The word "obedience" comes from the Greek word *hupakoe* and it means "an attentive hearing that leads to an active submission". An attentive hearing of what? An attentive hearing to the obedience of Christ. An attentive hearing of our blood-bought victory. When we hear and actively submit to our blood-bought identity and victory in Christ, we execute a devasting revenge attack on the devil. There is no sweeter revenge against the deceiver, the liar, the murderer, the thief, the destroyer than to walk in our blood-bought victory.

Every day for most of my adult life I would drive past the exact spot where my Father was shot. And every day as I passed that exact spot, it felt like a knife was being twisted inside me. I could never pass that place without a fresh burst of pain, anger and hate rising up within my soul and I hated it! So then one day as we were driving home, my wife Tracey asked me to park the car so that we could get some shopping. We parked the car and began to walk across the road to the shops. As we walked, our 5-year-old son, Reuben, took Tracey's and my hands and asked if we would "swing him" up into the air. We took his hands and proceeded to swing him high into the air. Each time Reuben landed he would shout "Boom!" as his feet touched the ground. We crossed the road and upon entering the shop God spoke to my heart. He said, "Turn around and look at where you gave Reuben that swing". I turned around and immediately warm tears began to flow as I realised the spot where we had given Reuben a swing was the exact spot where my Father was murdered, and I hadn't even noticed. There had been no fresh twist of the knife within me, no pain, no anger and no hatred. God again spoke to my heart, "You are free of it, son, you are no longer a victim but a victor. When you gave Reuben that swing, look at where his feet landed." The Spirit of God then shouted within me "BOOM! It's under Reuben's feet, because it's under his Daddy's feet. You are free Craig, son." As I stood amazed at God's good and gracious work in my life, God spoke up in my heart one more time. He said, "Enjoy your freedom and milk it for all it's worth, but know this, I have not just called you to freedom, I have called you to hit back. Satan tried to destroy you and your family, but it's your turn now."

As the Sons and Daughters of God it's our turn now! Embrace the revelation of your forgiveness in Christ and embrace the revelation of your justification in Christ. Let those revelations lead you to a place of innocence and from that place of innocence enter into a flow of authentic New Covenant repentance. And as part of that flow of repentance you get to exercise a godly vindication, a godly retaliation and revenge attack. The devil hates you with a fear-driven passion and because he hates you with a fear-driven passion, he hates to see you walking in your blood-bought victory. Your blood-bought victory outworked into every area of your life is your ultimate vindication and revenge.

In summary, let's reflect upon the cycle of authentic New Covenant transformation and change. You could call it the *methamorphoo* cycle. The key to walking free from sin and consistently walking in the good, acceptable and perfect will of God is the renovation of the mind. The key to the renovation of the mind, is authentic New Covenant repentance; *metanoia,* a change of mind that leads to a change of actions. Authentic New Covenant repentance flows from the inside out. Authentic New Covenant transformation begins with who you are inside, it begins with your inward man. The call to authentic New Covenant transformation is a call to be who you already are. Before God speaks to you about the sin that you are practicing, He desires to speak to you about who you are in Christ. Before God speaks to you about your wrong thinking which is driving your wrong doing, He desires to speak to you about your right being. God desires to first and foremost address you as a born-of-God, forgiven, justified, Son and Daughter of God. In so doing he will shut down satan's primary plan to take you to his courtroom to stand in guilt and activate the Father's plan to bring you into His throne room to sit in your innocence.

It's then from that place of innocence that a powerful flow of authentic New Covenant repentance will be activated, a flow that produces the following individual fruit:

Godly Sorrow

A sorrow that first and foremost consists of being sorry that you have grieved God. Secondly, a sorrow that consists of being sorry that you have been neglecting and missing out on the superior goodness of God.

Diligence

A glorious haste that is activated within your spirit-man, as you continue to feed on His goodness and soak in His presence. This self-same haste then floods into your soul causing you to move away from the sin that has been so easily ensnaring you at record-breaking speed.

Clearing of Yourselves

An open and honest manner that is free and clear of any form of excuse or self-defence. No more pretence, no more hiding, no more excuses, no more self-defence. Just a beautifully vulnerable clearing of yourself, in order to receive His amazing grace, His wisdom, His plan and His ability to rule and reign over all sin.

Indignation

A godly indignation and anger that arises from within your spirit. Not an anger that is fuelled by guilt and that leads to self-assassination. But an anger that is fuelled by grace and leads to the assassination of sin. An anger that has had enough of the self-harming that wounds and damages. An anger that attacks any sin that still ensnares you with the Kingdom weaponry of faith, hope and love. An anger that moves you into the good, acceptable and perfect will of God.

Fear

Not a fear of God or His judgment, but a fear of missing out on experiencing any aspect of His unmerited, unearned goodness for every area of your life. When you truly taste and experience His goodness it will cause you to tremble in awestruck wonder under the weight of His *checed*. When you truly taste and experience His goodness it will cause you to "clock" in His presence refusing to be moved because you are just to afraid of missing something.

Vehement Desire

A forceful and passionate longing for the goodness of God. A longing for the good acceptable and perfect will of God. A longing for His *soteria* made manifest in every area of your life.

Zeal

Purpose on fire. The fanning into flame and rekindling of the fire of your divine purpose.

Vindication

A retaliation and revenge attack. This last and powerful fruit of authentic New Covenant repentance, this vindication, is an attack against the deceiver, against the liar, against the thief that comes to steal, kill and destroy. It is against the devil himself. This retaliation and revenge attack is all about walking in your blood-bought victory, ruling and reigning in this life, over the curse, sickness, the devil and all of his demon cohorts. This is your retaliation. This is your revenge attack.

> The kingdoms of this world can only become the Kingdom of our Lord and of His Christ, in and through a powerful manifestation of the Sons and Daughters of God.

> The earth can only be filled with the knowledge of the glory of the Lord, as the waters cover the sea, in and through the self-same manifestation of the Sons and Daughters of God.

The manifestation of the Sons and Daughters of God can only come through a flow of Authentic New Covenant Transformation.

Authentic New Covenant Transformation can only come through a flow of Authentic New Covenant Repentance.

Authentic New Covenant Repentance can only flow from the solid foundational launching pad of *Your Justification*.

The foundational launching pad of your justification can only be truly built and established, from the foundation of *Your Forgiveness.*

The foundation of your forgiveness can only be truly built and established from the foundation of your *Spiritual Regeneration* (the revelation that *You Are Born of God*).

With all this in mind, I again invite you:

To feed and soak on the revelation of your *Spiritual Regeneration* (the revelation that You are *Born of God*), until it becomes a solid, established foundation in your life.

Then from the established foundation of your *Spiritual Regeneration*, feed and soak on the revelation of your *Forgiveness*, until it becomes a solid, established foundation in your life.

Then from the established foundation of your *Forgiveness*, feed and soak on the revelation of your *Justification*, until it becomes not only a solid, established foundation in your life, but a launching pad, from which the Spirit of Truth can propel you into an authentic flow of *New Covenant Repentance*.

Then in and from that flow of authentic *New Covenant Repentance*;
you will be transformed. You will be the seated reformer that God has called you to be. You will rule and reign in this life, over the curse, sickness and the devil. You will be a part of the manifestation of the Sons and Daughters of God that all creation is yearning for and you will see the goodness of God in the land of the living.

"For this reason a man shall leave his father and mother and be <u>joined</u> to his wife, and the two shall become one flesh." This is a great mystery, but I speak concerning Christ and the church.

Ephesians 5:31-32

CONCLUSION

I n conclusion, I encourage you to feed on the powerful truth of your spiritual regeneration, that you are born of God. Feed on the powerful truth of your forgiveness and justification, in Him. Don't just feed on them but soak them in His presence.

"For this reason a man shall leave his father and mother and be joined to his wife, and the two shall become one flesh." This is a great mystery, but I speak concerning Christ and the church.

Ephesians 5:31-32

The word "joined" comes from the Greek word *proskollao* and it means "to cleave". The word "mystery" comes from the Greek word *musterion* and it means "hidden secrets". The mysteries of our New Covenant are secrets hidden for us and not from us. The mystery of who we are in Christ, the mystery of how we come to walk in the fullness of Christ, the mystery of how we conceive all that we have been given in Christ, is hidden in the typology of a man cleaving to his wife. To be more specific one of the most vital aspects of biblical cleaving between a man and his wife is the flow of sexual intimacy. Religion would have you believe that the primary

God-ordained purpose for sexual intimacy between a man and his wife is conception. However, the primary God-ordained purpose for sexual intimacy between a man and his wife is not conception, but intoxication. The clear design of God is that intoxication precedes conception. In other words, the climax of cleaving is not conception but intoxication. The climax of faith is not conception but intoxication. I believe the primary cause of barrenness within the body of Christ when it comes to the conception of His great and precious promises, is a drive to conceive, whilst bypassing intoxication. I encourage you to study and feed on the truths within this book until they are soaked in His intoxicating presence. Feed on the glorious truth of your beloved identity, in Christ. Soak that truth in His intoxicating presence, until your heart is awakened to who you truly are.

Who Are You?

You are the Sons and Daughters of God

You have a Daddy

You are born of God

You are forgiven

You are justified

Sit in your innocence and repent

You are created for explosive and lasting change

Be the seated reformers

Be the reformation

Be the manifestation of the Sons and Daughters of God on the earth!

In Jesus' Name, Amen.

For further information about Seawright Ministries, podcasts and teachings please go to:

www.seawrightministiries.com

Printed in Poland
by Amazon Fulfillment
Poland Sp. z o.o., Wrocław